COGAT®
TEST PREP
GRADE 3 AND 4

- **2 MANUSCRIPTS**
- **COGAT® PRACTICE BOOK GRADE 3**
- **COGAT® TEST PREP GRADE 4**
- **LEVEL 9 AND 10 FORM 7**
- **516 PRACTICE QUESTIONS**
- **ANSWER KEY**
- **108 BONUS QUESTIONS ONLINE**

Nicole Howard

PLEASE LEAVE US A REVIEW!

Thank you for selecting this book.

We'd love to get your feedback on the website where you purchased this book.

By leaving a review, you give us the opportunity to improve our work.

Nicole Howard and The SkilledChildren.com Team

www.skilledchildren.com

Co-authors: Albert Floyd and Steven Beck

TABLE OF CONTENTS

INTRODUCTION

The Cognitive Abilities Test (CogAT®) is an assessment of a student's verbal, quantitative, and nonverbal reasoning ability. Administered to grades K-12, the CogAT® is designed to identify gifted students.

Riverside Publishing has developed the Cognitive Abilities Test since 1954.

These books will increase the student's chances of success by providing an overview of the different types of questions for Grade 3 and 4, Level 9 and 10, Form 7 of the CogAT® test.

Three practice tests (two for grade 3, one for grade 4) and their answer key, with clear explanations, are all included in each book to allow students to understand the testing structure and the different types of questions within it.

Additionally, by reading these books, you gain free online access to 108 bonus practice questions. You will find the link and password on the last page of each book.

It is highly recommended to read this introductory section to understand how the CogAT® works.

Which Students Are Eligible to Take the Levels 9/10?

These books are dedicated to gifted nine and ten-year-old children and therefore focus on level 9 and level 10, form 7 of CogAT®.

Most Grade 3/4 teachers implement CogAT® Level 9/10 to identify which of their students will benefit from faster curriculum training modules. Used as a starting evaluation, these tests deliver reasonably accurate results.

When in the School Year Does the CogAT® Take Place?

Several school districts choose to implement these tests at the end of the school year for more reliable and accurate results. If you are the parent or teacher of a student who could potentially qualify for this test, you will probably need to consult your school to determine how to enroll a child for this test.

An Overview of the CogAT® Level 9/10

The CogAT® is administered to a group of students at a single time.

There are three autonomous sections of the test, specifically:

1. Verbal testing

2. Nonverbal testing

3. Quantitative testing

These autonomous sections can be used individually, and some students may only be asked to take one or two parts of the test based on the evaluations of their tutors.

Although there are resources that support students prepare for these tests, the content of the CogAT® isn't generally the same content that is seen in the conventional school curriculum, and students will be asked to think creatively to solve certain questions.

The Length and the Complete Format of the Test

The total time given for the three sections of the Level 9/10 test is 90 minutes (30 minutes for each section).

Tests will vary, depending on the grades that are being assessed, but the Level 9 of CogAT® is divided into 170 multiple-choice questions. The Level 10 of CogAT® is divided into 176 multiple-choice questions. The questions are categorized as follows:

<u>Verbal Section</u>

- "Sentence completion" has 20 questions.

- "Verbal classification" has 20 questions.

- "Verbal analogies" has 24 questions for grade 4 and 22 questions for grade 3.

<u>Nonverbal Section</u>

- "Figure matrices" has 22 questions for grade 4 and 20 questions for grade 3.

- "Paper folding skills" has 16 questions.

- "Figure classifications" has 22 questions for grade 4 and 20 questions for grade 3.

<u>Quantitative Section</u>

- "Understanding number analogies" has 18 questions.

- "The number series" has 18 questions.

- "Solving number puzzles" has 16 questions.

The total number of questions for these three sections equals 176 for grade 4 and 170 for grade 3.

The Test Breakdown

The verbal section of the test is designed to assess a student's vocabulary, ability to solve problems associated with vocabulary, ability to determine word relationships, and their overall memory retention. The verbal section of the Level 9 and 10 of CogAT® has three subtypes of questions that need to be answered:

1. Sentence Completion: Students are required to select words that accurately complete sentences in this section. This tests their knowledge of vocabulary.

2. Verbal Classification: Students are required to classify words into like groups in this section. They will be given three words that have something in common, and will be asked to identify a fourth word that completes the set. Each question in this section will have five possible answers for the students to choose from.

3. Verbal Analogies: Students are required to identify analogies. They will be given two words that go together (e.g. "dog" and "mammal") as well as a third, unrelated word. They must pick the most fitting pair for the third word from the answer choices given, based on the logic used for the original pair of words.

The nonverbal section of the test is designed to assess a student's ability to reason and think beyond what they've already been taught. This section includes geometric shapes and figures that aren't normally seen in the classroom. This will force the students to use different methods to try and solve problems. There are also three subtypes of questions that need to be answered in the nonverbal section of the CogAT®:

1. Figure Classification: Students are required to analyze three similar figures and apply the next appropriate figure to complete the sequence in this section.

2. Figure Matrices: Students are introduced to basic matrices (2x2 grids) to solve for the missing shapes within them. Three of the four squares will already be filled out, and they must choose which image fills the last square from the options provided. This is similar to the verbal analogies section, except it is now done using shapes instead of words.

3. Paper Folding Skills: Students are introduced to paper folding and will need to ascertain where punched holes in a folded piece of paper would be after the paper is unfolded.

The quantitative section introduces abstract reasoning and problem-solving skills to learners and is one of the most challenging sections in the test. This section is also structured into three different parts:

1. Interpreting a Series of Numbers: Students are required to determine which number or numbers are needed to complete a series that follows a specific pattern.

2. Solving Number Puzzles: Students will need to solve number puzzles and simple equations. They will be provided with equations that are missing a number.

3. Understanding Number Analogies: Students are introduced to number analogies and will be required to determine what numbers are missing from the number sets. This is similar to figure matrices and verbal analogies.

How to Use the Content in These Books

Since the CogAT® is an important test in all students' schooling careers, the correct amount of preparation must be performed. Students that take the time to adequately prepare will inevitably do better than students that don't.

These books will help you prepare your student(s) before test day and will expose them to the format of the test so they'll know what to expect. These books include:

- Two full-length CogAT® Level 9 practice questionnaire.

- One full-length CogAT® Level 10 practice questionnaire.

- Question examples for teachers/parents to help their students approach all of the questions on the test with confidence and determination.

- Answer key for each book with clear explanations.

Take the time to adequately go through all of the sections to fully understand how to teach this information to younger students. Many of the abstract versions of these questions will be difficult for some students to understand, so including some visual aids during preparation times will be greatly beneficial.

Tips and Strategies for Test Preparation

The most important factor regarding the CogAT® is to apply the time and effort to the learning process for the test and make the preparation periods as stress-free as possible. Although everyone will experience stress in today's world, being able to cope with that stress will be a useful tool. All students will experience varying amounts of anxiety and stress before these types of tests, but one of the ways to adequately combat this is by taking the time to prepare for them.

The CogAT® has difficult questions from the very beginning. Some of the questions will range from difficult to very abstract, regardless of the age group or level.

It's necessary to encourage your students to use different types of strategies to answer questions that they find challenging.

Students will get questions incorrect in some of the sections, so it's vital to help younger students understand what errors they made so they can learn from their mistakes.

Before You Start Test Preparation

There are multiple factors that may stress students out, regardless of their age and maturity levels. It's imperative for you as an educator to help your students cope with the anxiety and stress of upcoming tests. The tests themselves are going to be stressful, but there are other, external factors that can increase the amounts of stress that children experience.

The first aspect that needs to be focused on is teaching the learners how to deal with stress. Breathing techniques are important, and having a quiet place to use when studying is imperative to decreasing the amount of stress that students experience.

There are other aspects that can help alleviate stress, like teaching your students what pens and pencils they need to bring on the test day and how to successfully erase filled out multiple-choice questions on the test questionnaire.

COGAT®PRACTICE BOOK GRADE 3

VERBAL BATTERY GRADE 3 TEST 1

This section is designed to assess a student's vocabulary, ability to solve problems associated with vocabulary, ability to determine word relationship and memory retention.

Verbal Analogies

A verbal analogy traces a similarity between a pair of words and another pair of words.

Example

dog → mammal : snake →

A reptile   **B** insect   **C** bird   **D** fish   **E** amphibian

- First, identify the relationship between the first pair of words.
- How do the words "dog" and "mammal" go together?

Scientists have classified the animals into classes to simplify their study.

Dog are mammals. "Mammal" is a category.

- Now, look at the word "snake".
- Which of the possible choices follows the previous rule?

Snake is a reptile, so the correct answer is A.

Tips for Solving Verbal Analogies

- Try to identify the correlation between the first two words.
- Review all answers before you make a choice.
- Remove any word in the answers that don't have a comparable kind of relationship.
- Also, evaluate the possible alternative meanings of the words.

1.
black → coal : white →

A bear   **B** horse   **C** rainbow   **D** snow
E apple

2.
hand → glove : foot →

A shoe   **B** hat   **C** head   **D** neck   **E** ear

3.
birds → sky : fishes →

A circus   **B** zoo   **C** sea   **D** snow   **E** desert

4.
left → right : horizontal →

A below   **B** middle   **C** down   **D** vertical
E diagonal

5.

all ➝ many : few ➝

A some   **B** never   **C** none   **D** always   **E** now

6.

hip ➝ ankle: shoulder ➝

A joint   **B** bone   **C** knee   **D** wrist   **E** head

7.

warm ➝ hot: old ➝

A new   **B** antique   **C** history   **D** years
E lower

8.

evening ➝ morning : dinner ➝

A time   **B** tea   **C** meal   **D** breakfast   **E** night

9.

butcher ⟶ knife : hairdresser ⟶

A hair   **B** scissors   **C** table   **D** blond   **E** grey

gray

10.

bow ⟶ arrow : bullet ⟶

A shoot   **B** protect   **C** gun   **D** iron   **E** steel

11.

child ⟶ human : poult ⟶

A horse   **B** bird   **C** canine   **D** snail   **E** frog

12.

bee ⟶ hive : bear ⟶

A honey   **B** lawn   **C** den   **D** stable   **E** hut

13.

bacteria → decomposition : yeasts →

A eruption   **B** fermentation   **C** cure   **D** fever
E disease

14.

palate → mouth : ceiling →

A room   **B** hill   **C** rainbow   **D** river   **E** sea

15.

bridge → river : tunnel →

A subway   **B** mountains   **C** road   **D** street
E path

16.

student → exam : employee →

A salary   **B** appraisal   **C** job   **D** promotion
E holiday

17.

patient → doctor : student →

A education   **B** teacher   **C** exam   **D** literacy
E training

18.

implausible → absurd : surprising →

mean what

A shocking   **B** important   **C** sweet   **D** happy
E new

19.

after → before : successor →

A tomorrow   **B** after   **C** predecessor   **D** before
E impostor

20.

pain → sedative : grief →

A joy   **B** fear   **C** pleasure   **D** consolation
E love

21.

archipelago → island : constellation →

A river   **B** flower   **C** star   **D** valley   **E** lake

22.

Europe → France: North America →

A Venezuela   **B** Chicago   **C** Guatemala
D Canada   **E** Spain

Verbal Classification

Verbal classification questions ask the student to choose the voice that belongs to a group of three words.

Example

apple, pear, banana

A cherry   **B** carrot   **C** lettuce   **D** garlic   **E** onion

- First, identify the relationship between the three words of the first row.
- What do the words apple, pear and banana have in common?

Apple, pear and banana are all fruit.

- Now, look at the five worlds: cherry, carrot, lettuce, garlic, onion. Which word goes best with the three words in the top row?

Cherry is also a fruit, so the correct answer is A.

Tips for Solving Verbal Classification Questions

- Try to identify the correlation between the three words in the top row.
- Review all answers before you make a choice.
- Remove every word in the answers that don't have any kind of relationship with the three words in the top row.
- Also, evaluate the possible alternative meanings of the words.

1.

leopard, cougar, lion

A elephant   **B** dog   **C** cat   **D** bear   **E** deer

2.

couch, chair, table

A rug   **B** bed   **C** lamp   **D** painting   **E** book

3.

cornea, retina, pupil

A vision   **B** sunglasses   **C** iris   **D** telescope
E microscope

4.

branch, leaf, root

A grass   **B** bark   **C** corn   **D** soil   **E** ground

5.

index, glossary, chapter

A book   **B** bibliography   **C** letter   **D** word
E magazine

6.

unimportant, trivial, insignificant

A trifling   **B** familiar   **C** absurd   **D** ridiculous
E nice

7.

core, seeds, pulp

A flower   **B** skin   **C** bark   **D** piece   **E** tree

8.

peninsula, cape, island

A bay   **B** ocean   **C** sea   **D** cliff   **E** river

9.

biology, chemistry, zoology

A theology   **B** zinc   **C** astronomy   **D** animal
E religion

10.

evaluate, assess, appraise

A estimate   **B** instruct   **C** dismiss **D** reply
E write

11.

water, tea, gasoline

A milk   **B** silk   **C** oxygen   **D** concrete   **E** gas

12.

seagull, swallow, eagle

A lion   **B** penguin   **C** cat   **D** dolphin   **E** bear

13.

dog, monkey, lion

A sparrow   **B** snake   **C** dolphin   **D** crab
E lobster

14.

Pacific, Atlantic, Indian

A Arctic   **B** Gulf of Mexico   **C** Greenland
D Ireland   **E** Mediterranean Sea

15.

snake, crocodile, lizard

A snail   **B** frog   **C** turtle   **D** bat   **E** worm

16.

car, truck, bike

A tractor   **B** cable car   **C** helicopter   **D** ship
E sled

17.

Chinese, Arabic, Italian

A Belgium **B** Italy **C** Brazil **D** China
E Spanish

18.

triangle, square, circle

A pyramid **B** pentagon **C** cube **D** sphere
E cone

19.

seeing, hearing, smelling

A closing **B** waiting **C** tasting **D** opening
E eating

20.

broccoli, lettuce, tomato

A carrot **B** apple **C** orange **D** strawberry
E cherry

Sentence Completion

Complete the phrase using the appropriate word that best fits the meaning of the sentence as a whole.

Example

The _____ man has grey hair and many wrinkles.

A old   **B** strong   **C** young   **D** amazing   **E** dangerous

- First, read the sentence. You will realize that one word is missing.
- Look at the answer choices under the main sentence. Which word would go better in the phrase?

Grey hair and many wrinkles suggest an old man. Therefore, the right choice is "A".

Tips for Sentence Completion

- First, read the incomplete phrase.
- Think about what type of word you can use and try to anticipate the answer.
- Remove every word in the answers that don't have any kind of relationship with the main sentence.
- Read the incomplete sentence again.

1.

The _____ woman has blonde hair and a beautiful skin.

A old   **B** strong   **C** young   **D** kind   **E** weak

2.

When the _____ Dachshund ran into the meadow, we could see his short legs.

A little   **B** big   **C** great   **D** fierce   **E** soft

3.

My teacher wants to _____ a school field trip to the zoo.

A calculate   **B** construct   **C** teach   **D** organize
E demolish

4.

Roger is studying for his exams and _____ takes a break because he is running out of time.

A often   **B** always   **C** seldom   **D** later   **E** now

5.

Bob _____ up all of the cake in one evening.

A disclosed   **B** gobbled   **C** removed
D collected   **E** bought

6.

If the weather is _____, the sun is shining and there is plenty of light.

A negative   **B** rainy   **C** bright   **D** dark
E progressive

7.

Jennifer is starting to get pretty _____ about the wedding.

A neutral   **B** tired   **C** basic   **D** excited   **E** bored

8.

Dr. Smith said the drug would continue to be used because it was _____ for most patients.

A toxic   **B** neutral   **C** safe   **D** bad   **E** hot

9.
Winter may seem like the ideal time to do interior painting, but it requires _____ ventilation.

A insufficient   **B** adequate   **C** hot   **D** few   **E** bad

10.
The pilot died because he didn't _____ medical treatment after the accident.

A refuse   **B** suspect   **C** visualize   **D** create
E accept

11.
Jack will only buy the motorcycle if his parents _____ his choice.

A access   **B** pay   **C** endorse   **D** refuse   **E** buy

12.

This is such a _____ town! There's nothing to do in the evenings.

A boring   **B** big   **C** modern   **D** nice   **E** new

13.

Nicole joined her husband in Moscow, but soon found life there bleak and _____.

A amazing   **B** beautiful   **C** stunning   **D** dismal
E standard

14.

Compared to its adult size, a newborn kangaroo is _____.

A new   **B** old   **C** funny   **D** minuscule   **E** nice

15.

This refrigerator is _____; it's time we bought a new one.

A new   **B** classical   **C** dirty   **D** big   **E** ancient

16.

It would be _____ for me to reveal anything my client has discussed with me.

A genuine   **B** popular   **C** unethical   **D** bad
E trustworthy

17.

France and Germany, once deadly _____, are now partners in the European Union.

A ally   **B** friend   **C** companions   **D** enemies
E patriots

18.

It's _____ how much work you can do in a day if you put your mind to it.

A huge   **B** true   **C** famous   **D** real   **E** amazing

19.

It is difficult to _____ what the long-term effects of the accident will be.

A start   **B** begin   **C** predict   **D** close   **E** fall

20.

Government departments are in direct _____ with each other for limited resources.

A friendship   **B** love   **C** hope   **D** demand
E competition

NON VERBAL BATTERY GRADE 3 TEST 1

This section is designed to assess a student's ability to reason and think beyond what they've already been taught. This section includes geometric shapes and figures that aren't normally seen in the classroom.

Figure Matrices

Students are provided with a 2X2 matrix with the image missing in one cell. They have to identify the relationship between the two spatial shapes in the upper line and find a fourth image that has the same correlation with the left shape in the lower line.

Example

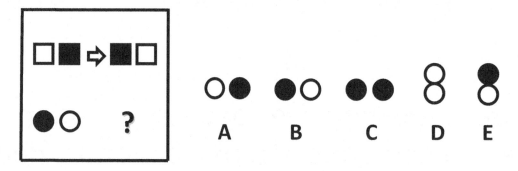

In the upper left box, the image shows a white square and a black square. In the upper right box, the image shows the same squares, but now the white square follows the black square.

The lower left box shows a black circle and a white circle. Which answer choice would go with this image in the same way as the upper images go together?

The image of the answer choice must show two circles but in opposite positions compared to the figures on the left. In other words, the black circle must follow the white circle.
The right answer is "A".

Tips for Figure Matrices

- Consider all the answer choices before selecting one.
- Try to use logic and sequential reasoning.
- Eliminate the logically wrong answers to restrict the options.
- Train yourself to decipher the relationship between different figures and shapes.

1.

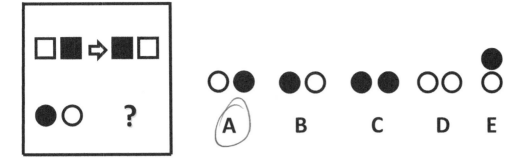

2.

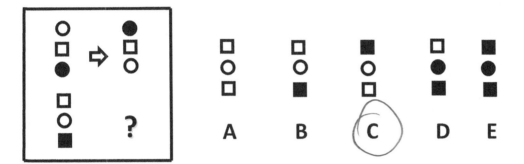

3.

4.

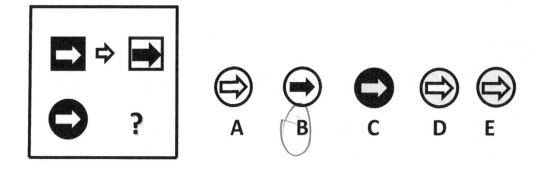

5.

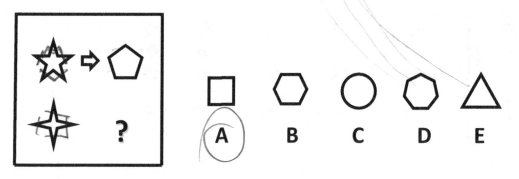

6.

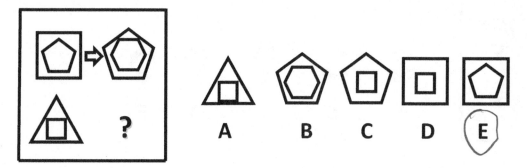

7.

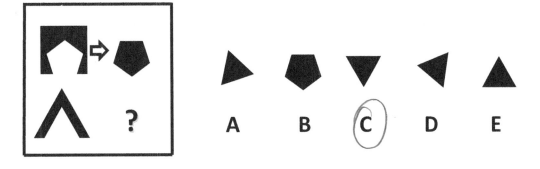

8.

9.

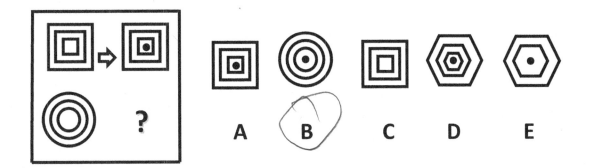

10.

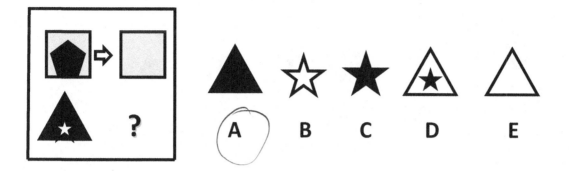

11.

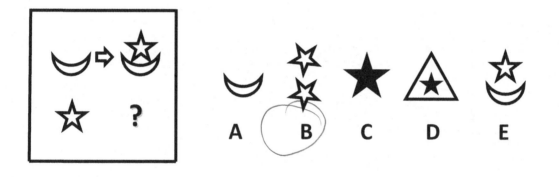

12.

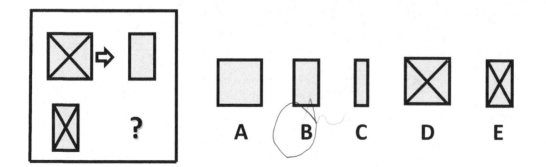

13.

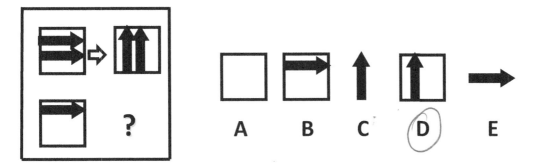

A   B   C   D   E

14.

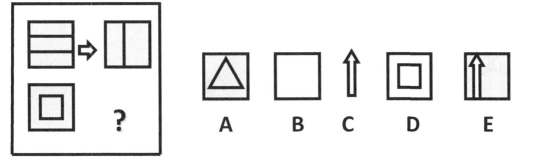

A   B   C   D   E

15.

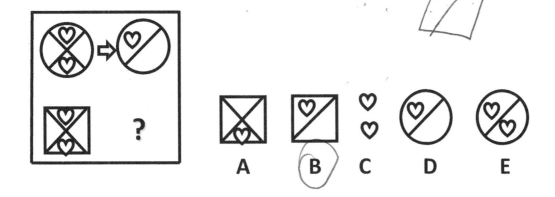

A   B   C   D   E

16.

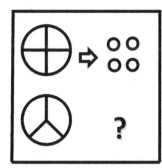

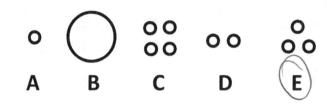

17.

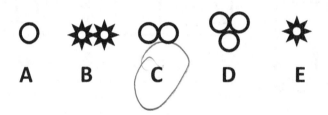

18.

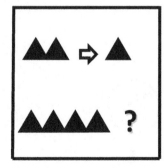

19.

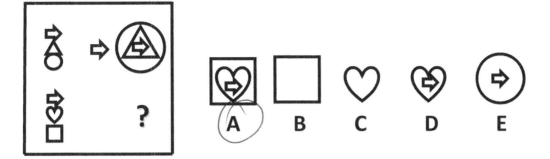

A   B   C   D   E

20.

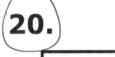

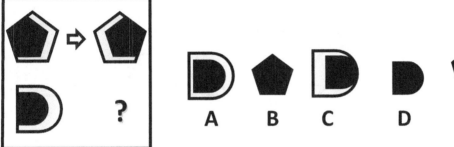

A   B   C   D   E

Figure Classification

Students are provided with three shapes and they have to select the answer choice that should be the fourth figure in the set, based on the similarity with the other three figures. The intention is to test the student's ability to recognize similar patterns and to make a rational choice.

Example

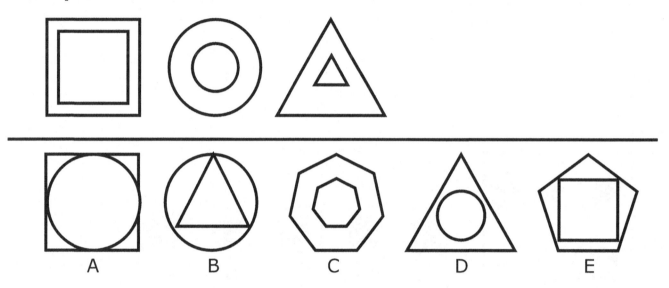

Look at the three pictures on the top. What do these three figures have in common?

You can see a square in a bigger square, a circle in a bigger circle, a triangle in a bigger triangle.

Now, look at the shapes in the row of the answer choices. Which image matches best the three shapes in the top row?

The image of the answer choice must show two identical figures, the smaller one inside the larger one. The right answer is "C" (a smaller heptagon in a larger heptagon).

Tips for Figure Classification

- Be sure to review all answer choices before selecting one.
- Try to use logic and sequential reasoning.
- Try to exclude the obviously wrong options to reduce the answer choices.

1.

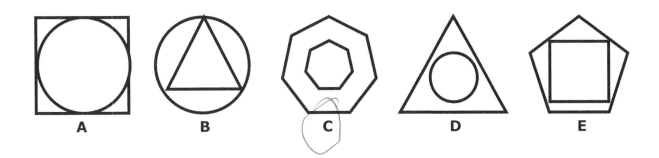

2.

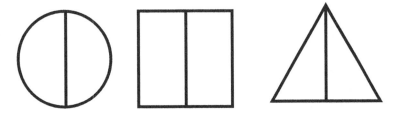

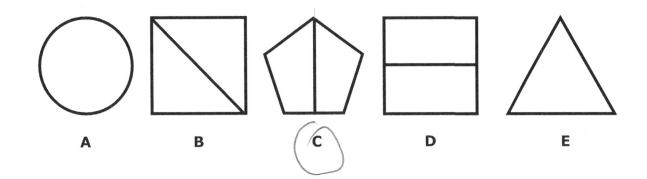

3.

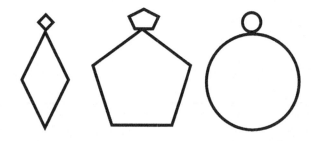

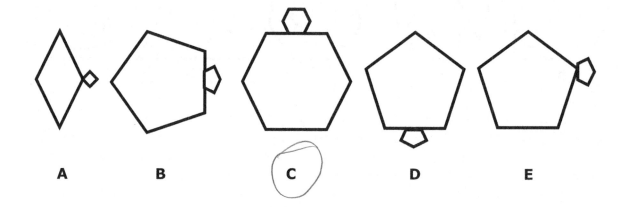

A   **B**   **C**   **D**   **E**

4.

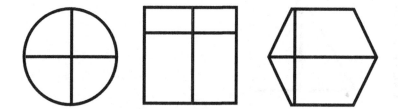

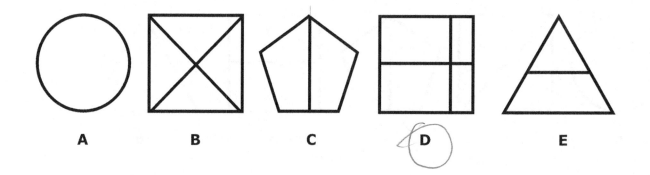

A   **B**   **C**   **D**   **E**

5.

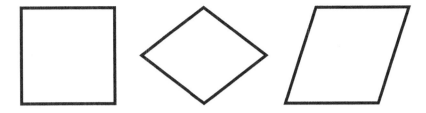

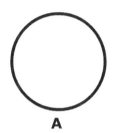    

A   B   C   D   E

6.

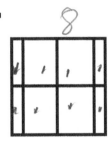  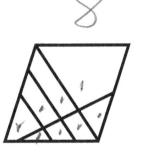

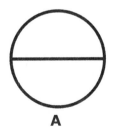  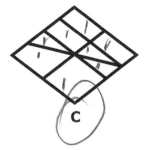  

A   B   C   D   E

7.

 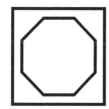 

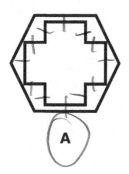    

A B C D E

8.

 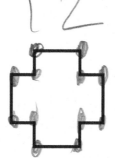 

A B C D E

9.

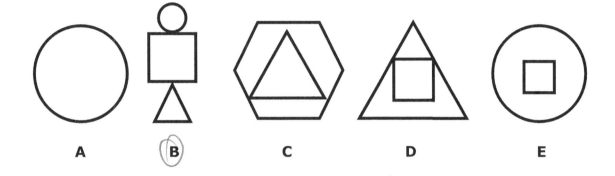

10.

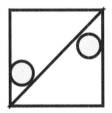  

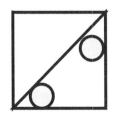  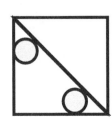 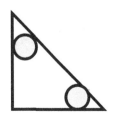 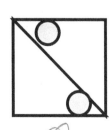

A   B   C   D   E

11.

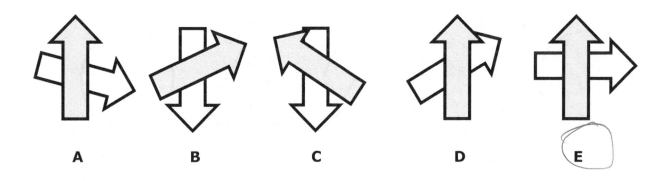

A	B	C	D	E

12.

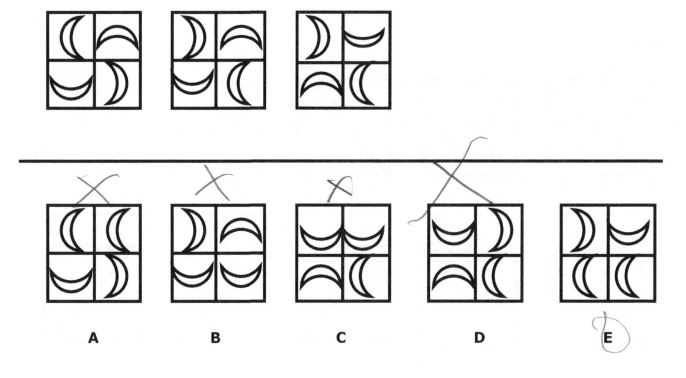

A	B	C	D	E

13.

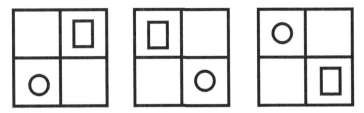

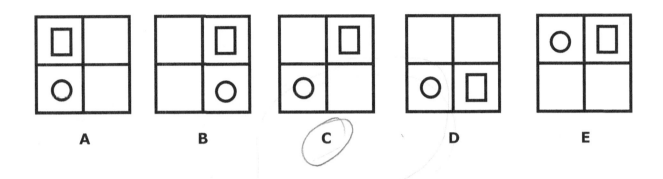

| A | B | C | D | E |

14.

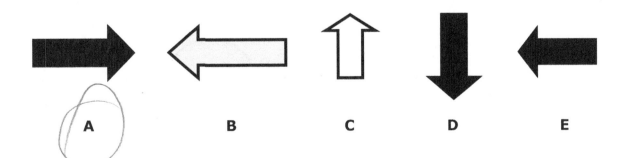

| A | B | C | D | E |

15.

A   B   C   D   E

16.

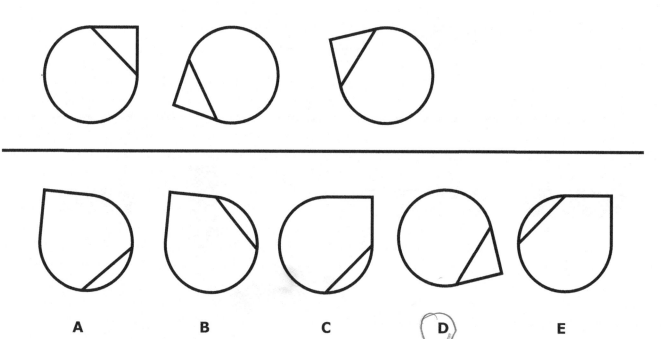

A   B   C   D   E

17.

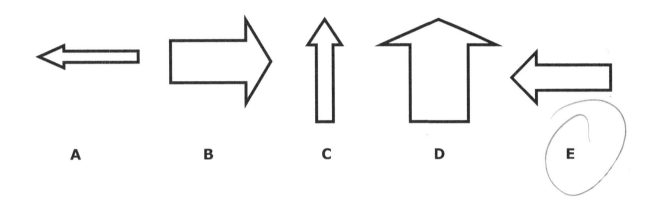

A   B   C   D   E

18.

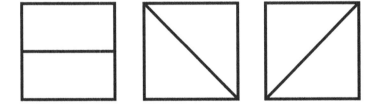

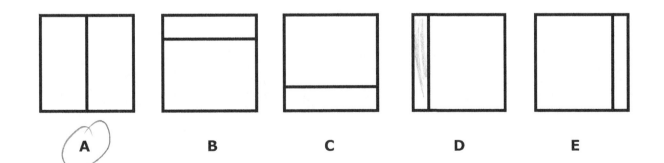

A   B   C   D   E

19.

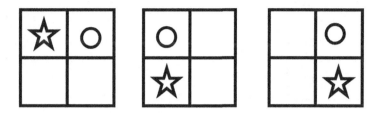

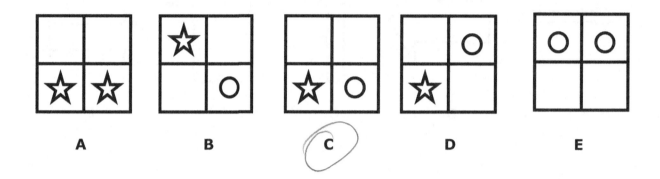

| A | B | C | D | E |

20.

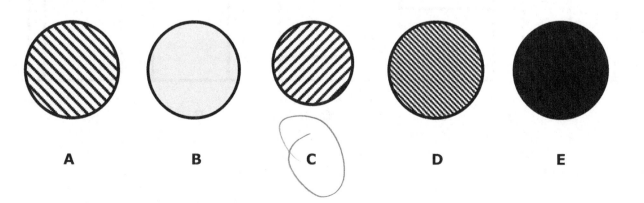

| A | B | C | D | E |

Paper Folding

Students need to determine the appearance of a perforated and folded sheet of paper, once opened.

Example

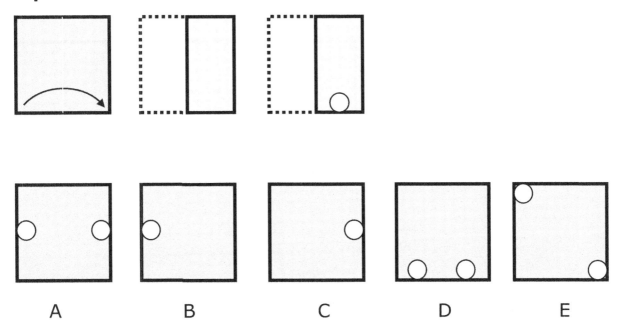

The figures at the top represent a square piece of paper being folded, and the last of these figures has one hole on it.

One of the lower five figures shows where the perforation will be when the paper is fully unfolded. You have to understand which of these images is the right one.

First, the paper was folded horizontally, from left to right.

Then, one hole was punched out. Therefore, when the paper is unfolded the hole will mirror on the left and right side of the sheet.

The right answer is "D".

Tips for Paper Folding

The best way to get ready for these challenging questions is to practice. The patterns that show up on the test can confuse students, so the demonstration of folding and unfolding real paper can be very helpful.

1.

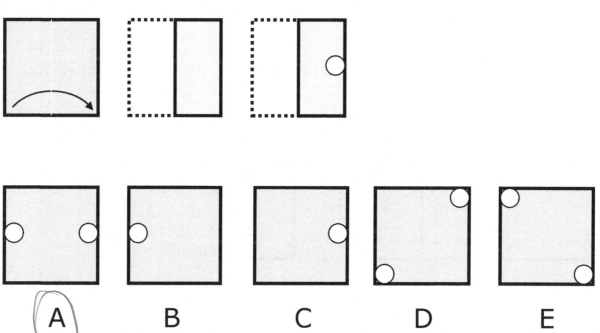

2.

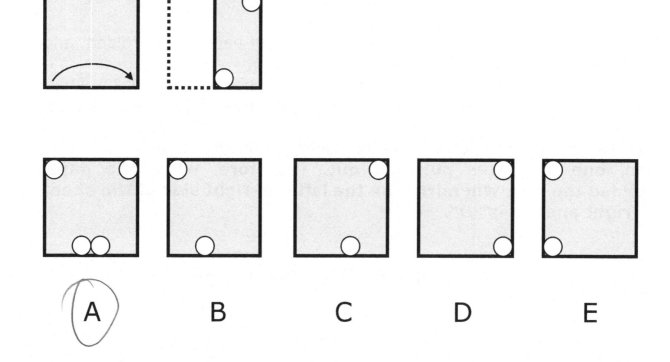

3.

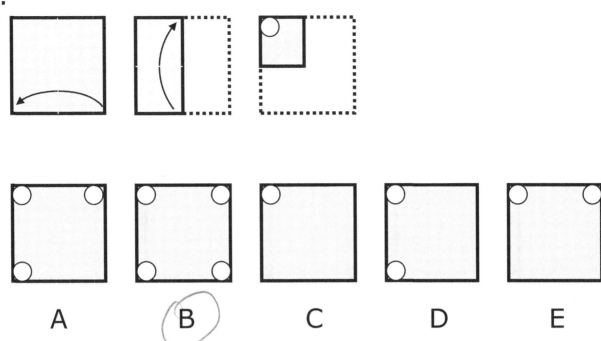

A   B   C   D   E

4.

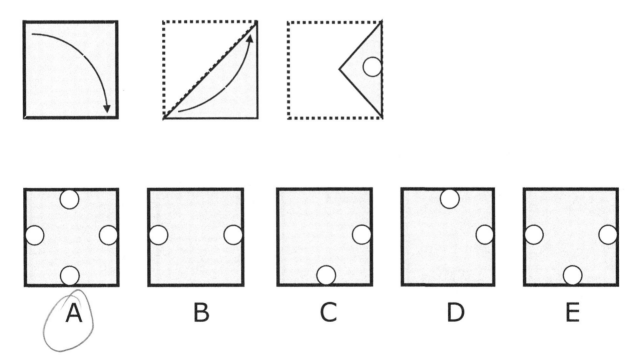

A   B   C   D   E

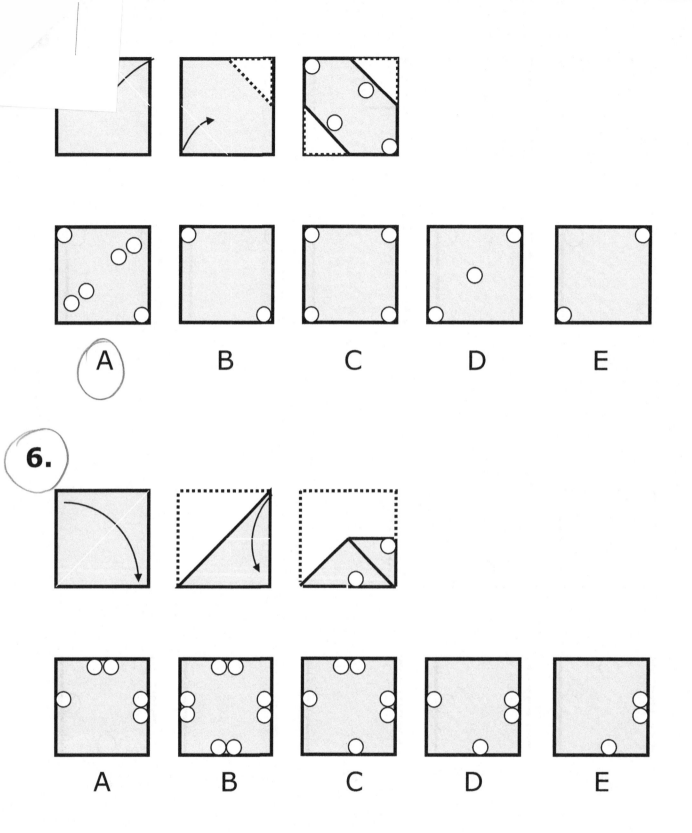

7.

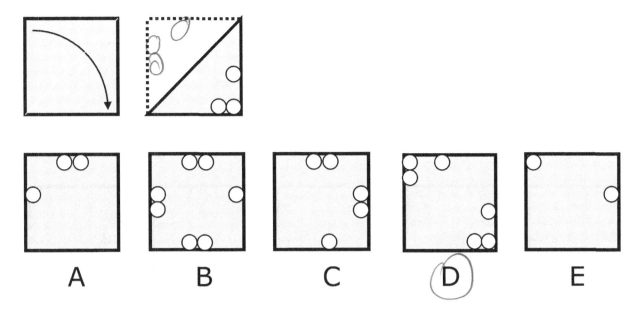

8.

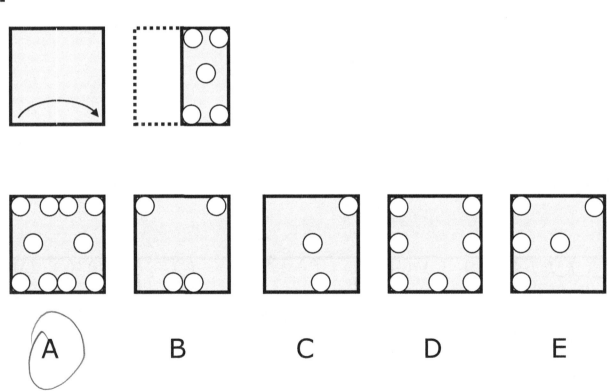

9.

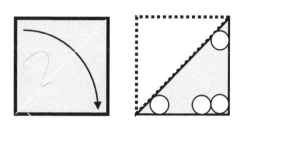

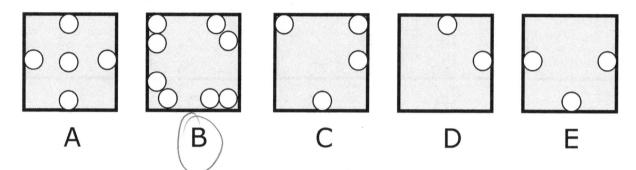

A   B   C   D   E

10.

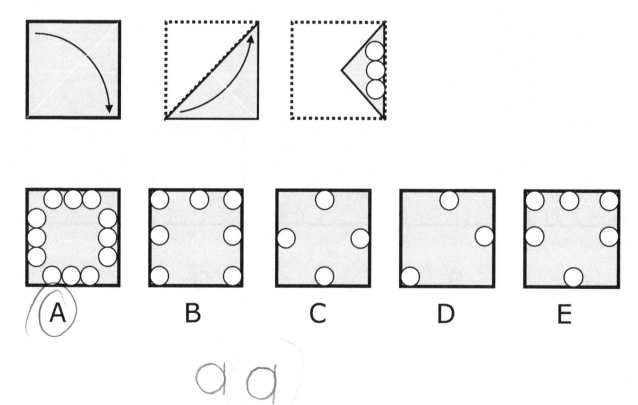

A   B   C   D   E

11.

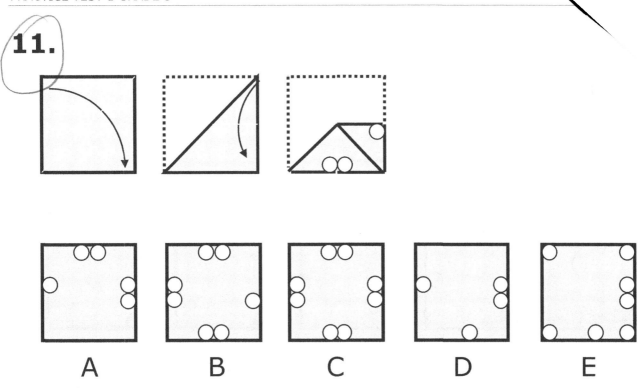

12.

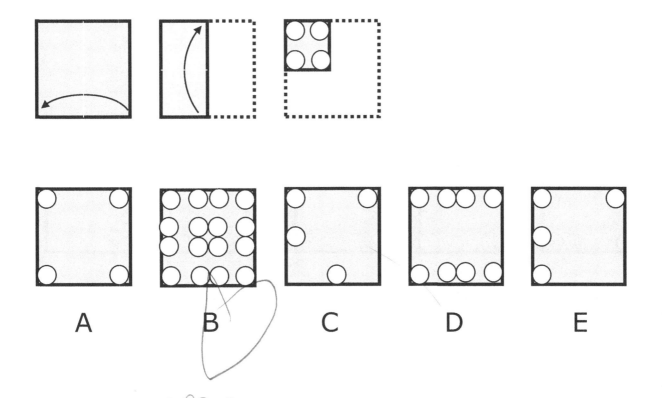

PRACTICE

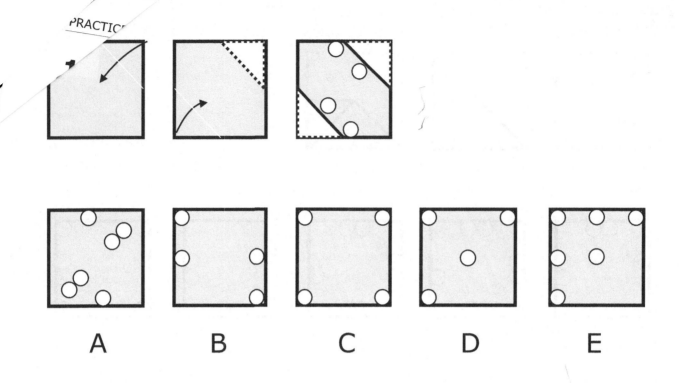

A   B   C   D   E

14.

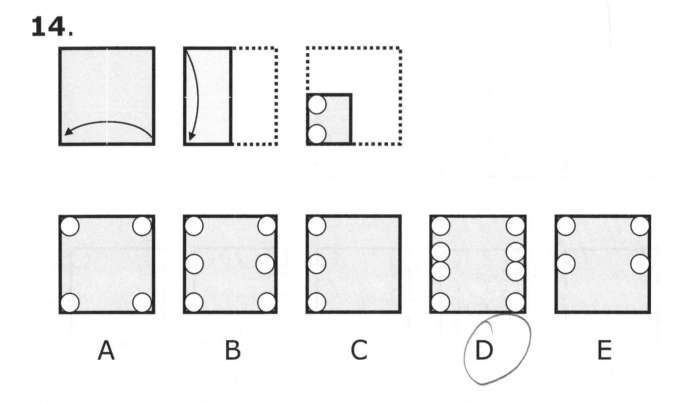

A   B   C   D   E

15.

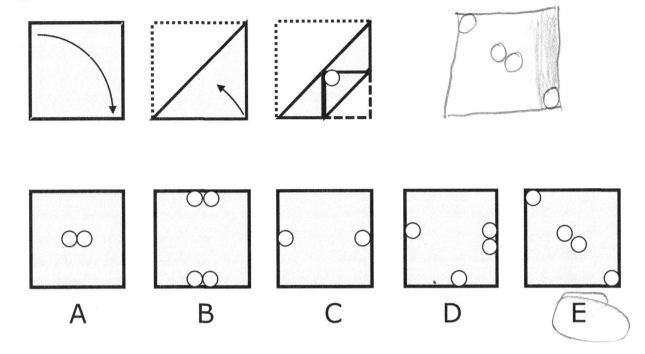

16.

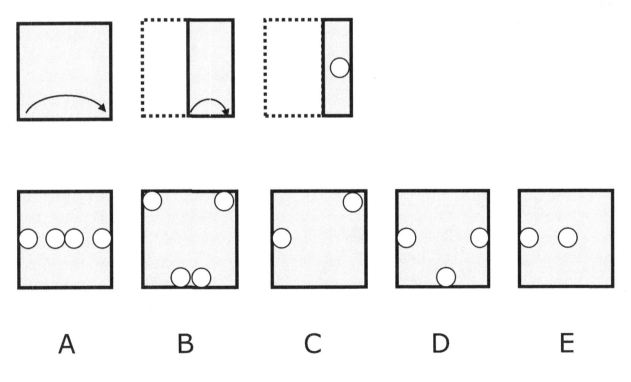

QUANTITATIVE BATTERY GRADE 3 TEST 1

This section introduces abstract reasoning and problem-solving skills to learners and is one of the most challenging sections in the test.

Number Puzzle

Students are required to solve basic mathematical equations. An equation says that two things are equal. It will have an equals sign "=" like this:

$$4 + 2 = 10 - 4$$

The equation says that what is on the left (4 + 2) is equal to what is on the right (10 − 4).

Example 1

$$? - 15 = 4$$

A 10   B 19   C 1   D 7   E 16

- The right side of the equal sign is 4. Which answer should be given in place of the question mark, so that the left side of the equal is also 4?
$$19 - 15 = 4; 4=4$$
The right answer is "B".

Example 2

$$? + \blacklozenge = 10$$

$$\blacklozenge = 5$$

A 1   **B** 13   **C** 5   **D** 8   **E** 9

? + 5= 10; 5+5=10; 10=10; the right answer is "C".

Tips for Number Puzzle

- Deeply understand the meaning of "equal", as the purpose is to provide the missing information that will make the two parts of the equation the same.
- Train yourself to solve simple basic equations.
- Practice with numbers and problem solving.

1.

$$? - 6 = 4$$

A 10   **B** 11   **C** 14   **D** 7   **E** 16

2.

$$? + \blacklozenge = 10$$

$$\blacklozenge = 5$$

A 1   **B** 13   **C** 5   **D** 8   **E** 9

3.

$$? + 2 = \blacklozenge$$

$$\blacklozenge = 6$$

A 0   **B** 4   **C** 11   **D** 2   **E** 10

4.

$$? \times 3 = \blacklozenge + 1$$

$$\blacklozenge = 5$$

A 10   **B** 9   **C** 2   **D** 4   **E** 6

5.

$$? - 3 = \blacklozenge + 1$$

$$\blacklozenge = 9$$

A 20   **B** 1   **C** 3   **D** 12   **E** 13

6.

$$20 + 12 = 45 - ?$$

A 2   **B** 13   **C** 30   **D** 6   **E** 1

7.

$$90 = 100 - 3 - ?$$

A 7   **B** 20   **C** 4   **D** 8   **E** 1

8.

$$25 = 50 - 27 + ?$$

A 10   **B** 4   **C** 1   **D** 6   **E** 2

9. $$88 = 25 + 43 + ?$$

A 30   **B** 29   **C** 24   **D** 20   **E** 12

10.

$$78 - 21 = 89 - ?$$

A 229   **B** 2   **C** 20   **D** 32   **E** 14

11.

$$23 + 19 = 45 - ?$$

A 3   **B** 7   **C** 2   **D** 10   **E** 8

12.

$$64 - 18 = 98 - ?$$

A 8 **B** 52 **C** 25 **D** 34 **E** 55

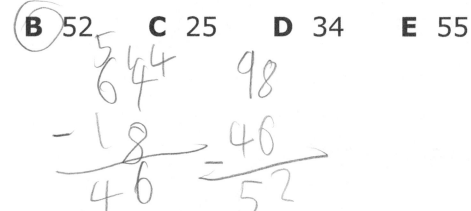

13.

$$? = \blacklozenge + 46$$

$$\blacklozenge = 25$$

A 41 **B** 30 **C** 69 **D** 50 **E** 71

14.

$$? = \blacklozenge \times 7$$

$$\blacklozenge = 5$$

A 3 **B** 10 **C** 35 **D** 27 **E** 30

15.

$$? = \blacklozenge \times 7$$

$$\blacklozenge = 8$$

A 69   **B** 56   **C** 54   **D** 55   **E** 43

16.

$$? = \blacklozenge + 7$$

$$13 = \blacklozenge - \bullet$$

$$\bullet = 4$$

A 25   **B** 15   **C** 24   **D** 2   **E** 19

Number Analogies

In this session, you will see two pairs of numbers and then a number without its pair. The first two pairs of numbers are correlated in some way. Try to find out the correlation between the numbers within each of the pairs. Choose an answer that gives you the third pair of numbers, related to each other in the same way.

Example

[9 → 18]   [5 → 14]   [15 → ?]

A 20   **B** 18   **C** 24   **D** 7   **E** 16

- In the first two sets, you have 9 and 18; 5 and 14. Both numbers (9 and 5), increase by 9 (9+9=18; 5+9=14).
- Apply the same rule to the number 15.

15 + 9 = 24. The right answer is "C".

Tips for Number Analogies

- Step 1: acquire all the information from the two given pairs (relationships, sums, subtractions, etc.).
- Step 2: apply the same rules, relations, formulas that you correctly identified in step 1.
- Step 3: double-check that the rule has been properly applied.

1.

[9 → 12]   [5 → 8]   [15 → ?]

A 20   **B** 18   **C** 11   **D** 7   **E** 16

2.

[5 → 10]   [8 → 16]   [3 → ?]

A 6   **B** 10   **C** 14   **D** 9   **E** 13

3.

[13 → 10]   [8 → 5]   [15 → ?]

A 3   **B** 12   **C** 11   **D** 5   **E** 9

4.

[10 → 5]   [8 → 4]   [18 → ?]

A 12   **B** 10   **C** 5   **D** 9   **E** 24

[5 → 12]   [3 → 8]   [11 → ?]

A 10   **B** 6   **C** 12   **D** 9   **E** 24

6.

[5 → 40]   [8 → 64]   [3 → ?]

A 24   **B** 10   **C** 12   **D** 3   **E** 16

7.

[5 → 14]   [1 → 2]   [3 → ?]

A 1   **B** 15   **C** 8   **D** 15   **E** 20

8.

[20 → 11]   [35 → 26]   [11 → ?]

A 12   **B** 14   **C** 3   **D** 2   **E** 21

9.

[15 → 8]   [30 → 23]   [11 → ?]

A 4   **B** 10   **C** 30   **D** 2   **E** 25

10.

[23 → 27]   [31 → 35]   [25 → ?]

A 11   **B** 1   **C** 3   **D** 24   **E** 29

11.

[20 → 24]   [35 → 39]   [11 → ?]

A 2   **B** 19   **C** 15   **D** 2   **E** 26

12.

[8 → 40]   [2 → 10]   [10 → ?]

A 50   **B** 10   **C** 3   **D** 20   **E** 2

13.

[18 → 6]   [36 → 12]   [6 → ?]

A 14   **B** 1   **C** 30   **D** 2   **E** 11

14.

[20 → 8]   [35 → 23]   [19 → ?]

A 11   **B** 19   **C** 7   **D** 2   **E** 21

15.

[9 → 6]   [22 → 19]   [50 → ?]

A 50   **B** 47   **C** 30   **D** 2   **E** 22

16.

[28 → 4]   [35 → 5]   [63 → ?]

A 1   **B** 12   **C** 30   **D** 9   **E** 20

17.

[24 → 3]   [32 → 4]   [8 → ?]

A 1   **B** 13   **C** 3   **D** 10   **E** 20

18.

[20 → 38]   [35 → 68]   [11 → ?]

A 1   **B** 20   **C** 30   **D** 2   **E** 12

$$\begin{array}{r} 35 \\ -\ 12 \\ \hline 23 \end{array}$$

Number Series

Students are provided with a sequence of numbers that follow a pattern. They are required to identify which number should come next in the sequence.

Example 1

$$2 \qquad 6 \qquad 10 \qquad 14 \qquad ?$$

A 18   **B** 11   **C** 10   **D** 7   **E** 16

- It's easy to realize that each number in the sequence increases by 4. 2+4=6; 6+4=10; 10+4=14; etc.
- Apply the same rule to the number 14.

14 + 4 = 18. The right answer is "A".

Example 2

$$2 \qquad 8 \qquad 5 \qquad 11 \qquad 8 \qquad ?$$

A 1   **B** 10   **C** 12   **D** 6   **E** 14

- The sequence follows the rule: +6, -3, +6, -3, +6, etc. 2+6=8; 8-3=5; 5+6=11; 11-3=8; etc.
- Apply the same rule to the number 8.

8 + 6 = 14. The right answer is "E".

Tips for Number Series

- To correctly answer these questions, the student will need to be able to identify the patterns in a sequence of numbers and provide the missing item. Therefore, it is important to practice, working with sequences of numbers.

1.

    2   **6**   **10**   **14**   **?**

A 18   **B** 11   **C** 10   **D** 7   **E** 16

2.

    5   **4**   **3**   **2**   **1**   **?**

A 12   **B** 10   **C** 0   **D** 7   **E** 13

3.

    4   **10**   **7**   **13**   **10**   **?**

16 13 19 16

A 1   **B** 10   **C** 12   **D** 6   **E** 16

4.

+5 −4 +5 −4 +5 −4 +5

    1   **6**   **2**   **7**   **3**   **8**   **4**   **?**

A 3   **B** 9   **C** 6   **D** 10   **E** 12

5.

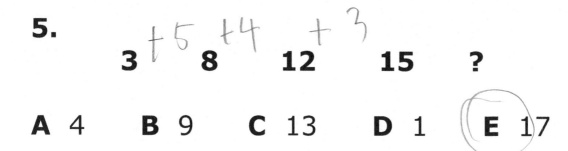

3   8   12   15   **?**

A 4   **B** 9   **C** 13   **D** 1   **E** 17

6.

1   0   3   2   5   4   **?**

A 2   **B** 4   **C** 7   **D** 6   **E** 9

7.

3   0   3   0   3   **?**

A 1   **B** 2   **C** 3   **D** 5   **E** 0

8.

9   6   7   4   5   2   **?**

A 1   **B** 2   **C** 3   **D** 5   **E** 0

9.

33   28   23   18   13   ?

A 8   **B** 5   **C** 30   **D** 10   **E** 2

10.

2   3   5   6   8   9   ?

A 8   **B** 2   **C** 24   **D** 9   **E** 11

11.

7   9   14   16   21   23   ?

A 2   **B** 28   **C** 21   **D** 3   **E** 15

12.

3   6   2   5   1   4   ?

A 1   **B** 0   **C** 2   **D** 3   **E** 9

13.

41   44   44   47   47   50   ?

A 9   **B** 10   **C** 29   **D** 3   **E** 50

14.

0.5   1.5   2.5   3.5   4.5   5.5   ?

A 0.1   **B** 6.5   **C** 0.35   **D** 4.5   **E** 1.5

15.

0.02   0.07   0.12   0.17   0.22   ?

A 0.03   **B** 0.1   **C** 0.35   **D** 0.27   **E** 0.3

16.

77   66   55   44   33   22   ?

A 11   **B** 14   **C** 6   **D** 50   **E** 71

17.

41   **50**   **59**   **68**   **77**   **86**   **?**

A 68   **B** 76   **C** 69   **D** 95   **E** 73

18.   +1.5   +1.5 +1.5   1.5

2   **3.5**   **5**   **6.5**   **8**   **9.5**   **?**

A 11   **B** 1.5   **C** 12   **D** 12.5   **E** 1

VERBAL BATTERY GRADE 3 TEST 2

Verbal Analogies

1.
yellow ➞ lemon : red ➞

A frog   **B** dog   **C** blood   **D** grass   **E** sun

2.
wrist ➞ watch : neck ➞

A ring   **B** chain   **C** hat   **D** gloves   **E** pin

3.
earthquake ➞ tsunami: heavy rain ➞

A flood   **B** river   **C** sea   **D** snow   **E** beach

4.
sunrise ➞ dawn : sunset ➞

A below   **B** middle   **C** day   **D** dusk   **E** night

5.
small → dwarf: big →

A woman   **B** man   **C** giant   **D** little   **E** few

6.
heat → cooked: cold →

A chilly   **B** ice cream   **C** snow   **D** frozen
E snow

7.
pinch → pain: hug →

A massage   **B** comfort   **C** hurt   **D** squeeze
E eat

8.
sniff → smell : lick →

A eat   **B** taste   **C** stink   **D** run   **E** sleep

9.

tired ➝ sleep : hungry ➝

A drink   **B** sleep   **C** fall   **D** wake up   **E** eat

10.

orator ➝ speak : singer ➝

A scream   **B** sing   **C** walk   **D** smell   **E** cry

11.

white ➝ black ➝ up

A after   **B** down   **C** before   **D** tomorrow
E always

12.

airplane ➝ air : ship ➝

A desert   **B** water   **C** fire   **D** sand   **E** oil

13.
kind → cruel : happy →

A talented   **B** smart   **C** sad   **D** new   **E** big

14.
chapter → book : fender →

A room   **B** automobile   **C** hammer   **D** door
E page

15.
mirror → smooth : sandpaper →

A bad   **B** big   **C** rough   **D** old   **E** soft

16.
knife → cut : shovel →

A dig   **B** smile   **C** pack   **D** create   **E** pull

17.

fish: → sea : moose →

A house   **B** desert   **C** sea   **D** forest   **E** ocean

18.

chuckle → laugh : whimper →

A speak   **B** cry   **C** complain   **D** repeat   **E** smile

19.

carpenter → wood : plumber →

A ropes   **B** pipes   **C** pitons   **D** sticks   **E** lamps

20.

author → write : chef →

A eat   **B** create   **C** cook   **D** destroy   **E** close

21.

zoologist → animals : botanist →

A plants   **B** fishes   **C** stars   **D** roses
E planets

22.

sculptor → statue : poet →

A pen   **B** poem   **C** imagine   **D** dream   **E** paper

Verbal Classification

1.

man, monkey, macaque

A dolphin   **B** penguin   **C** cat   **D** lemur   **E** dog

2.

copper, zinc, aluminum

A bronze   **B** plastic   **C** silk   **D** cardboard
E paper

3.

eye, nose, mouth

A legs   **B** arms   **C** neck   **D** shoulders   **E** ears

4.

beak, wing, tail

A trunk   **B** scales   **C** feathers   **D** teeth   **E** gills

5.
parrot, bat, crow

A penguin   **B** turkey   **C** chicken   **D** ostrich
E eagle

6.
Italy, Spain, France

A Egypt   **B** Syria   **C** Atlantic   **D** Greece
E Ghana

7.
allow, permit, let

A ask   **B** start   **C** close   **D** consent   **E** shut

8.
snow, rain, hail

A sand   **B** water   **C** sleet   **D** moon   **E** river

9.

beat, hit, strike

A knock   **B** choose   **C** pick   **D** ask   **E** request

10.

brave, courageous, valiant

A intelligent   **B** heroic   **C** poor   **D** rich   **E** nice

11.

parallelogram, rectangle, square

A cube   **B** triangle   **C** circle   **D** pyramid
E rhombus

12.

incorporate, comprise, include

A come   **B** arrive   **C** contain   **D** make
E safeguard

13.

shark, trout, salmon

A whale   **B** dolphin   **C** penguin   **D** snake
E blue marlin

14.

Mediterranean, Caribbean, Caspian

A Artic   **B** Baltic   **C** Pacific   **D** Indian
E Atlantic

15.

bee, fly, ant

A woodlice   **B** millipede   **C** scorpion   **D** butterfly
E worm

16.

elephant, goat, gazelle

A cow   **B** lion   **C** wolf   **D** hyena   **E** leopard

17.
lamp, candle, fire

A Jupiter   **B** Sun   **C** Earth   **D** book   **E** wind

18.
demand, claim, require

A obtain   **B** search   **C** need   **D** buy   **E** desire

19.
door, window, balcony

A chair   **B** furniture   **C** sofa   **D** roof   **E** garden

20.
fulfill, realize, accomplish

A forbid   **B** ban   **C** reach   **D** finish   **E** discover

Sentence Completion

1.

Standing in the doorway was a _____ woman with long black hair and green eyes.

A ugly   **B** old   **C** beautiful   **D** silly   **E** new

2.

A _____ fire destroyed more than thirty homes.

A massive   **B** little   **C** black   **D** fierce   **E** new

3.

These instruments _____ distances precisely.

A form   **B** calculate   **C** know   **D** organize
E receive

4.

Miss Taylor confessed that she had _____ wanted to visit the States.

A seldom **B** always **C** tomorrow **D** now **E** later

5.

She wanted to arrive feeling cool, calm, and _____.

A disclosed **B** removed **C** destroyed **D** collected
E tired

6.

I have washed your shirt but it is still _____.

A negative **B** wet **C** bright **D** new **E** old

7.

People are _____ of hearing politicians make promises that they never keep.

A neutral **B** tired **C** excited **D** amazed
E bored

8.

Research has found that the drug contains a _____ chemical that can cause respiratory problems.

A toxic **B** safe **C** old **D** amazing **E** big

9.

There has been _____ rainfall over the past two years, and farmers are having trouble.

A bad **B** adequate **C** large **D** many **E** insufficient

10.

They _____ the idea because it would cost too much money.

A accepted **B** suspected **C** created **D** found
E rejected

11.

I absolutely _____ to take part in anything illegal.

A accept **B** access **C** try **D** sell **E** refuse

12.

Mathematics is becoming increasingly important in its applications and uses in the _____ world.

A boring **B** old **C** modern **D** simple **E** small

13.

The industry _____ of temperature for shipping products is 41 degrees Fahrenheit.

A range   **B** stop   **C** type   **D** list   **E** standard

14.

Darwin published his _____ work on evolution in 1859.

A weak **B** strong **C** funny **D** little **E** monumental

15.

Migrating birds cover _____ distances every winter.

A little   **B** super   **C** immense   **D** partial
E ancient

16.

If a student has _____ objections to a school activity, they don't have to participate.

A genuine   **B** bad   **C** unethical   **D** new
E trustworthy

17.

Mum and Dad didn't seem to approve much of my new _____.

A ally   **B** parents   **C** companions   **D** enemies
E workers

18.

The United States is a _____ country with a relatively thin population spread over it.

A huge   **B** little   **C** new   **D** real   **E** amazing

19.

I can't find my passport. It must have _____ out of my pocket.

A started   **B** fallen   **C** predicted   **D** closed
E dropped

20.

Opinion polls show that the voters have lost _____ in the administration.

A time **B** fear **C** confidence **D** demand **E** money

NON VERBAL BATTERY GRADE 3
TEST 2

Figure Matrices

1.

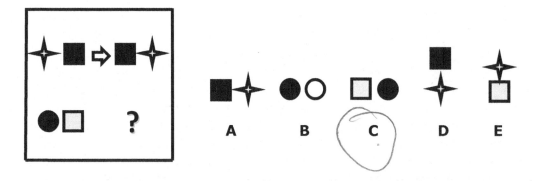

2.

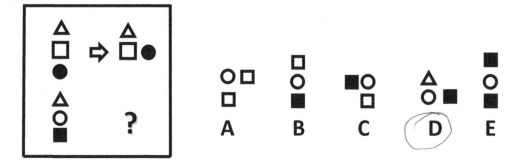

3.

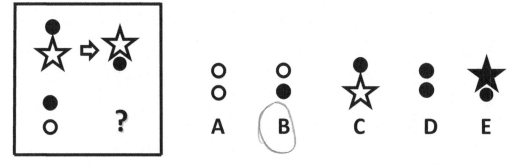

4.

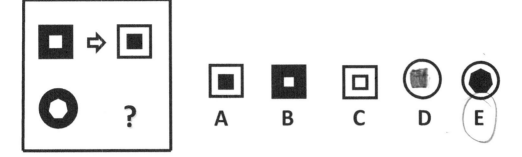

A   **B**   **C**   **D**   **E**

5.

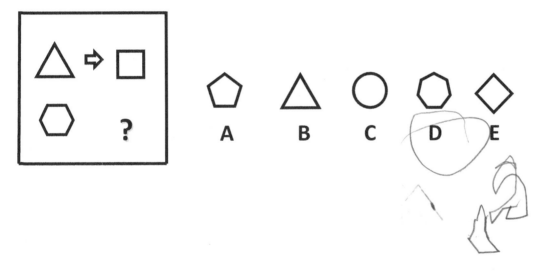

A   **B**   **C**   **D**   **E**

6.

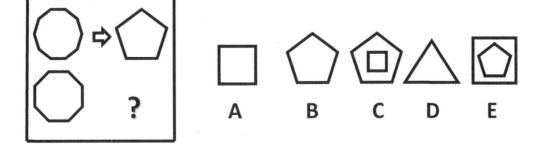

A   **B**   **C**   **D**   **E**

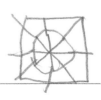

7.

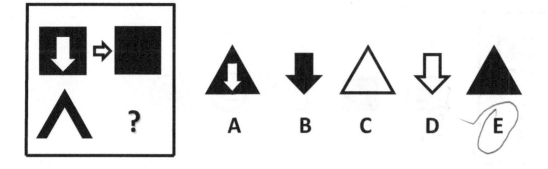

8.

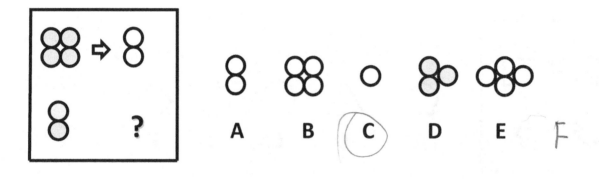

9.

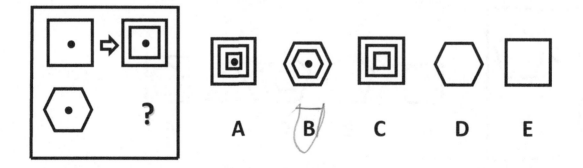

10.

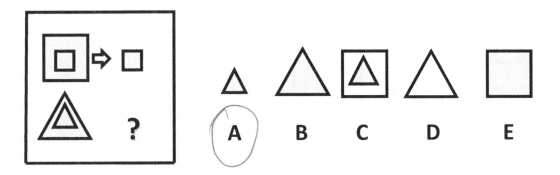

11.

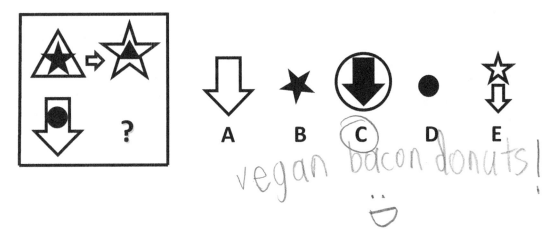

vegan bacon donuts!

12.

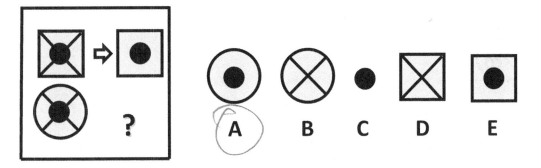

13.

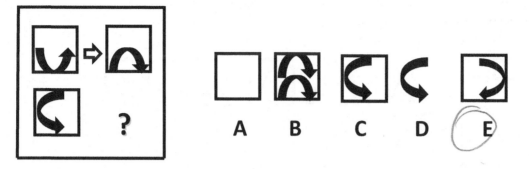

14.

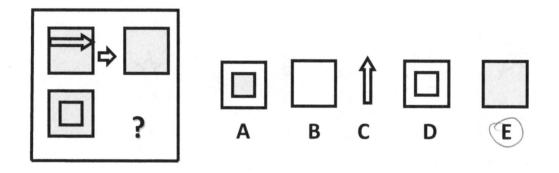

15.

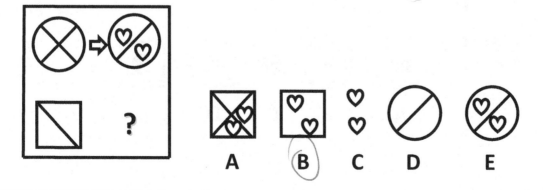

16.

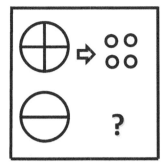

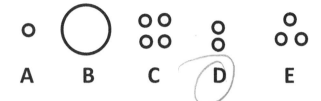

A   B   C   D   E

17.

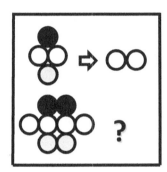

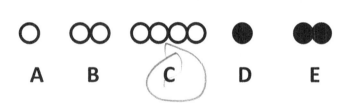

A   B   C   D   E

18.

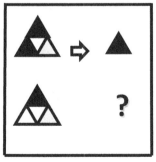

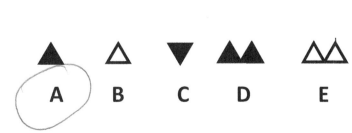

A   B   C   D   E

19.

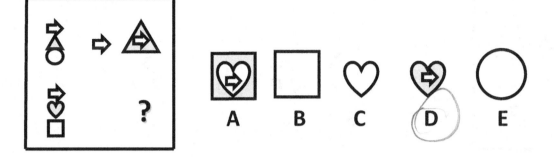

20.

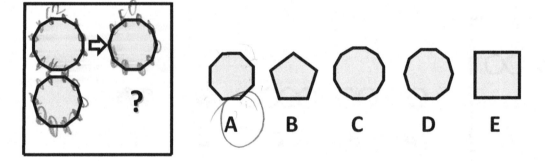

Figure Classification

1.

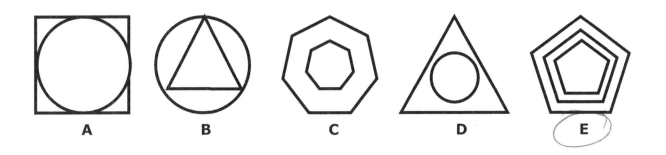

2.

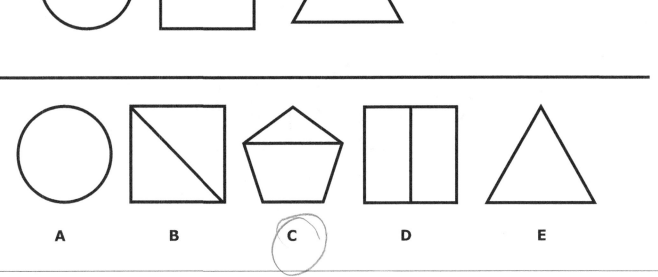

3.

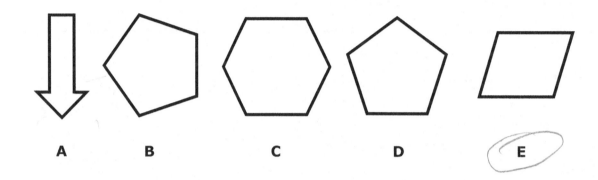

| A | B | C | D | E |

4.

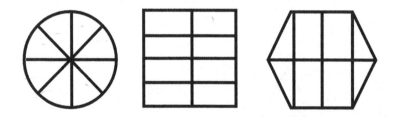

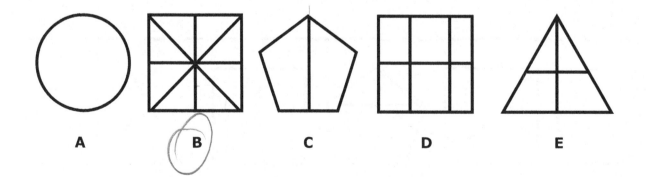

| A | B | C | D | E |

5.

A   **B**   **C**   **D**   **E**

6.

    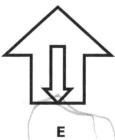

A   **B**   **C**   **D**   **E**

7.

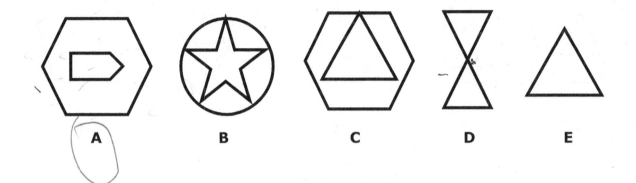

8.

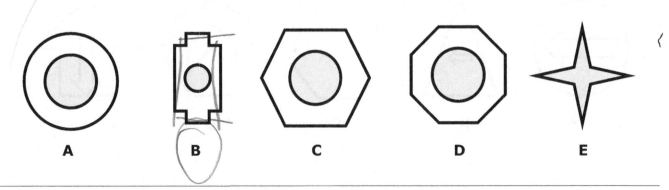

9.

A	B	C	D	E

10.

  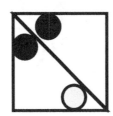 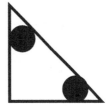 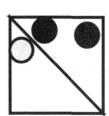

A	B	C	D	E

11.

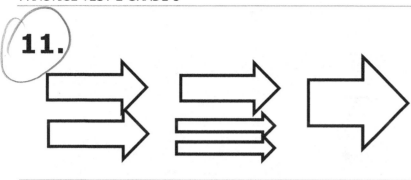

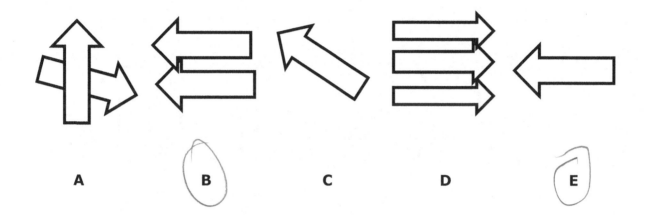

A   B   C   D   E

12.

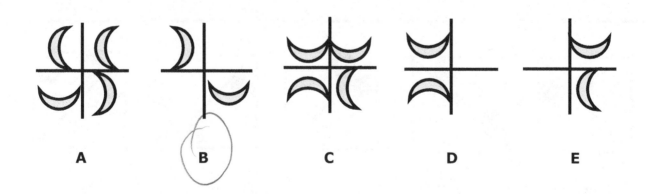

A   B   C   D   E

13.

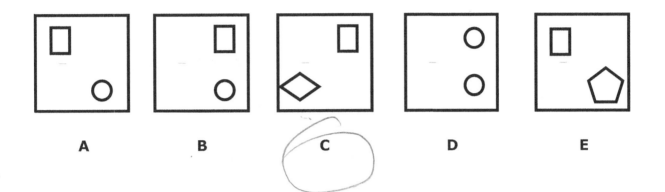

14.

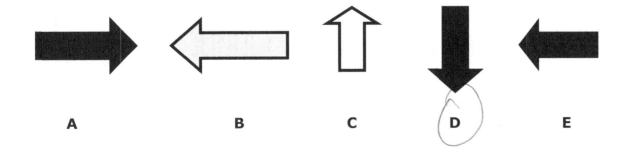

15.

   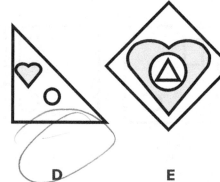

| A | B | C | D | E |

16.

| A | B | C | D | E |

17.

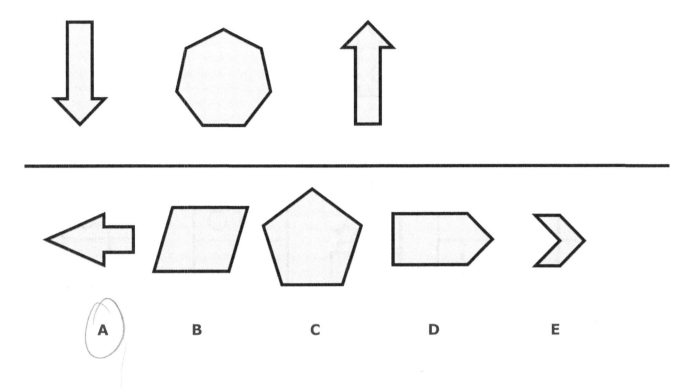

A   B   C   D   E

18.

A   B      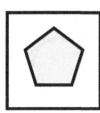   E

C   D

19.

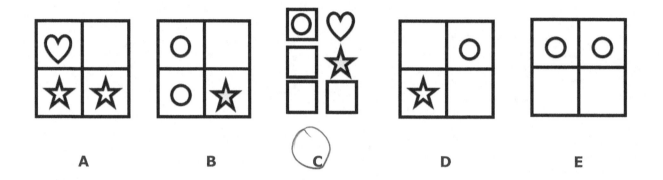

A   B   C   D   E

20.

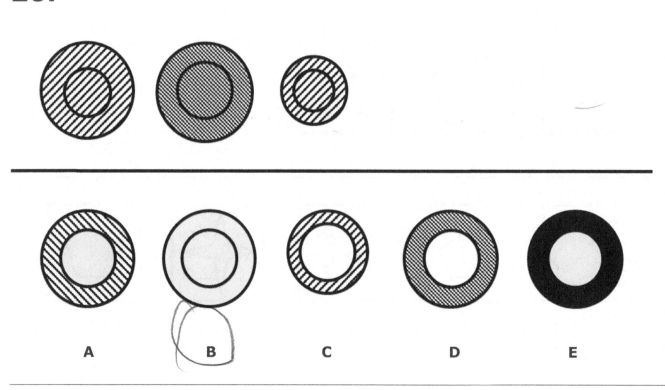

A   B   C   D   E

Paper Folding

1.

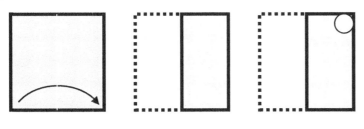

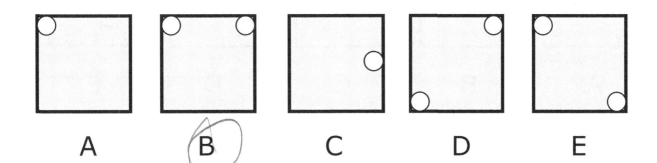

A B C D E

2.

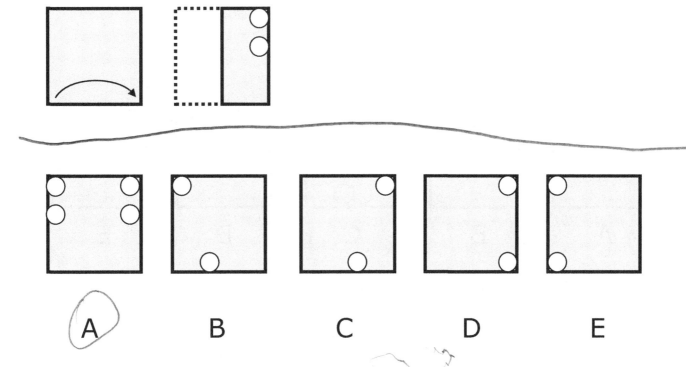

A B C D E

3.

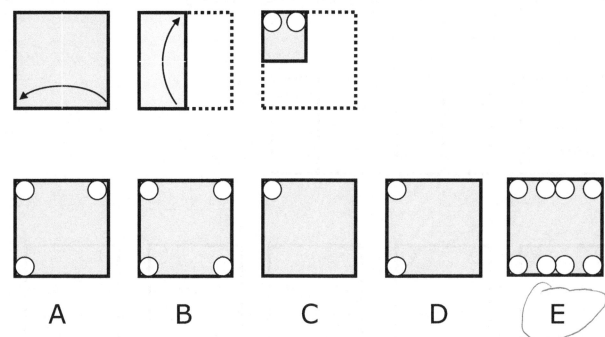

4.

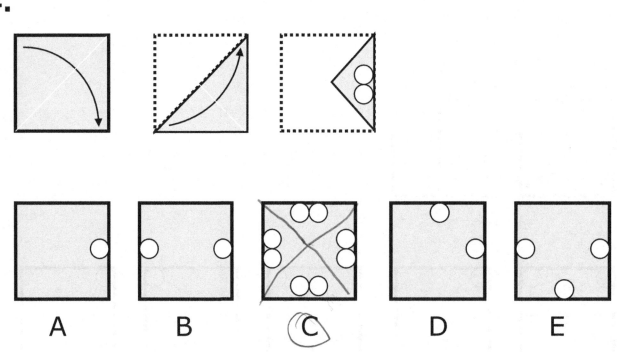

5.

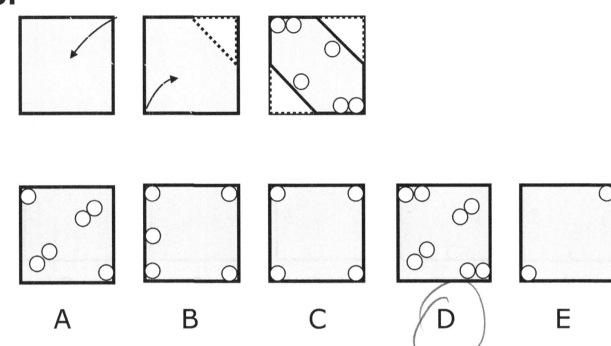

A   B   C   D   E

6.

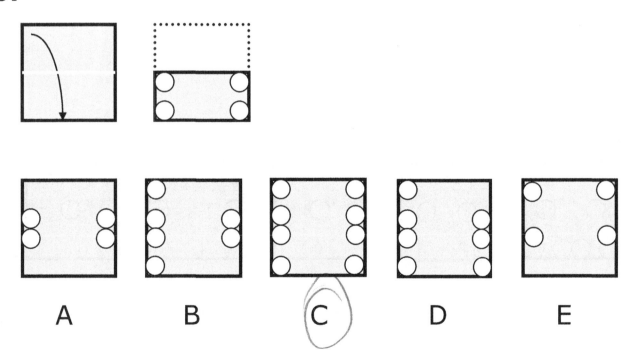

A   B   C   D   E

7.

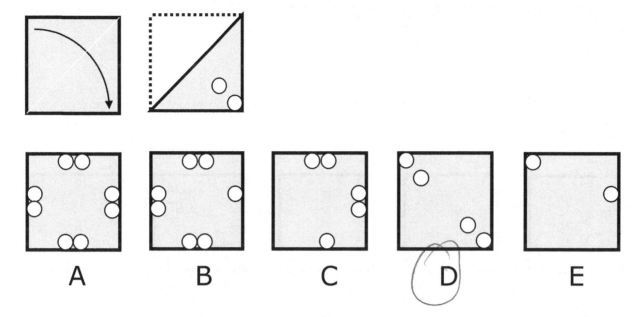

A   B   C   D   E

8.

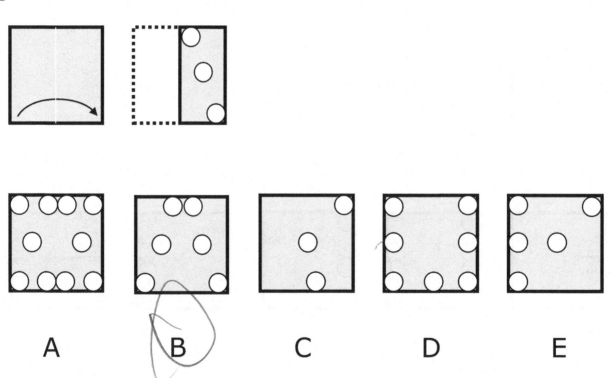

A   B   C   D   E

9.

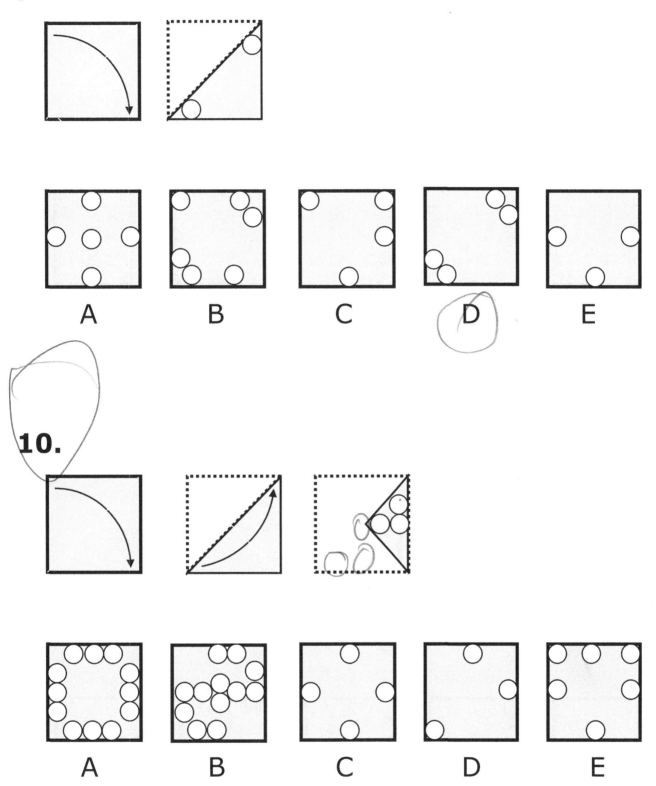

A B C D E

10.

A B C D E

11.

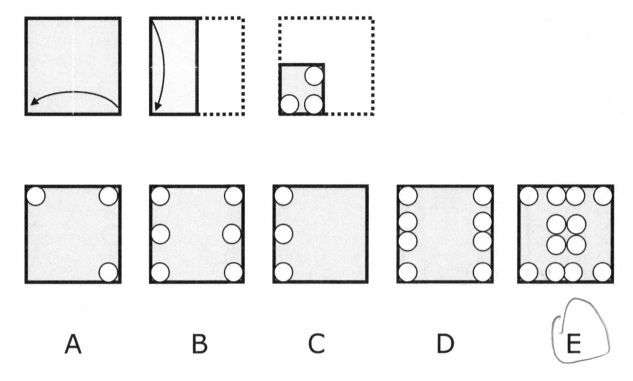

12.

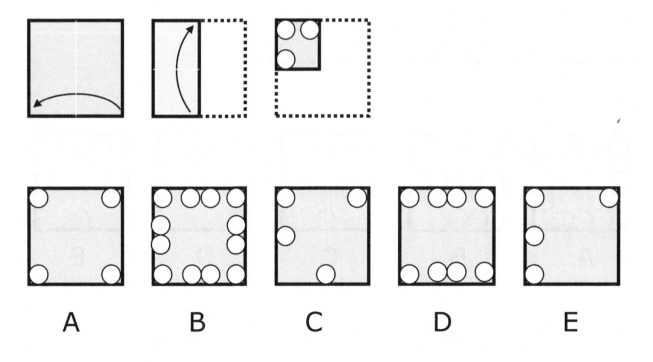

13.

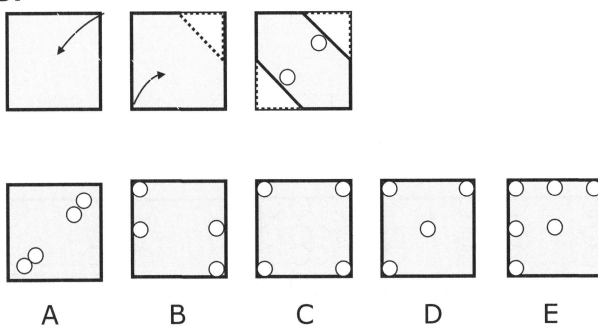

A   B   C   D   E

14.

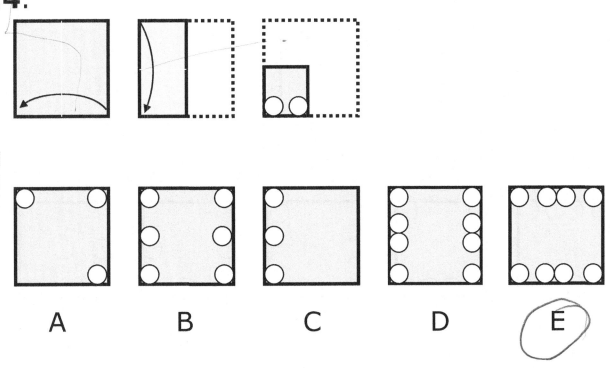

A   B   C   D   E

15.

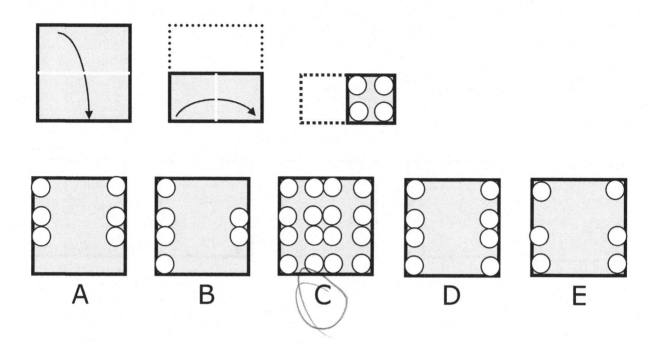

A   B   C   D   E

16.

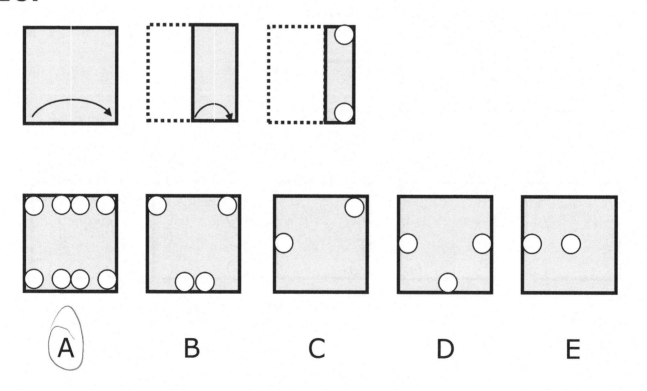

A   B   C   D   E

QUANTITATIVE BATTERY GRADE 3
TEST 2

Number Puzzle

1.

? - 11 = 13

A 24   **B** 10   **C** 142   **D** 7   **E** 11

2.

? + ◆ = 15

◆ = 9

A 2   **B** 6   **C** 50   **D** 7   **E** 1

3.

? + 2 = ◆

◆ = 10

A 2   **B** 40   **C** 10   **D** 1   **E** 8

4.

$$? \times 2 = \blacklozenge + 1$$

$$\blacklozenge = 9$$

A 11   **B** 5   **C** 2   **D** 3   **E** 7

5.

$$? - 3 = \blacklozenge + 1$$

$$\blacklozenge = 21$$

A 21   **B** 11   **C** 3   **D** 25   **E** 22

6.

$$33 + 14 = 50 - ?$$

A 20   **B** 12   **C** 30   **D** 2   **E** 3

7.

$$90 = 100 - 3 - ?$$

A 7   **B** 11   **C** 20   **D** 80   **E** 1

8.

$$32 = 51 - 40 + ?$$

A 11   **B** 21   **C** 22   **D** 60   **E** 20

9. $$66 = 12 + 27 + ?$$

A 27   **B** 29   **C** 21   **D** 18   **E** 11

10.

$$92 - 33 = 61 - ?$$

A 21   **B** 2   **C** 1   **D** 3   **E** 19

46

11.

$$29 + 17 = 62 - ?$$

A 16   **B** 70   **C** 21   **D** 8   **E** 4

69

12.

$$78 - 9 = 92 - ?$$

A 80   **B** 5   **C** 23   **D** 31   **E** 54

13.

$$? = \blacklozenge + 12$$

$$\blacklozenge = 10$$

A 40   **B** 3   **C** 22   **D** 51   **E** 70

14.

$$? = \blacklozenge \times 7$$

$$\blacklozenge = 9$$

A 2   **B** 11   **C** 33   **D** 21   **E** 63

15.

$$? = \blacklozenge \times 21$$

$$\blacklozenge = 2$$

A 42   **B** 51   **C** 54   **D** 33   **E** 40

16.

$$? = \blacklozenge + 29$$

$$5 = \blacklozenge - \bullet$$

$$\bullet = 1$$

A 24   **B** 16   **C** 21   **D** 35   **E** 18

Number Analogies

1.

[9 → 14]   [5 → 10]   [15 → ?]

A 20   **B** 18   **C** 11   **D** 7   **E** 15

2.

[4 → 8]   [8 → 16]   [14 → ?]

A 10   **B** 6   **C** 28   **D** 9   **E** 14

3.

[10 → 7]   [6 → 3]   [12 → ?]

A 5   **B** 11   **C** 10   **D** 4   **E** 9

4.

[6 → 2]   [12 → 4]   [18 → ?]

A 12   **B** 11   **C** 6   **D** 9   **E** 2

5.

[5 → 11]   [3 → 9]   [11 → ?]

A 11   **B** 6   **C** 12   **D** 17   **E** 21

6.

[6 → 42]   [8 → 56]   [3 → ?]

A 21   **B** 11   **C** 12   **D** 30   **E** 12

7.

×3
−1

×3
−1

[6 → 17]   [1 → 2]   [4 → ?]

A 2   **B** 14   **C** 11   **D** 18   **E** 2

8.

[20 → 13]   [35 → 28]   [50 → ?]

A 145   **B** 18   **C** 30   **D** 43   **E** 21

9. =11

[19 → 8]   [30 → 19]   [11 → ?]

A 0   **B** 11   **C** 3   **D** 2   **E** 29

10. +4

[19 → 23]   [29 → 33]   [21 → ?]

A 10   **B** 18   **C** 3   **D** 20   **E** 25

11. +6

[21 → 27]   [32 → 38]   [11 → ?]

A 1   **B** 17   **C** 15   **D** 2   **E** 22

12.

[7 → 35]   [3 → 15]   [20 → ?]

A 100   **B** 10   **C** 30   **D** 80   **E** 20

13.

[15 → 5]   [33 → 11]   [9 → ?]

A 12   **B** 10   **C** 3   **D** 20   **E** 1

14.

[22 → 10]   [34 → 22]   [13 → ?]

A 1   **B** 18   **C** 3   **D** 20   **E** 15

15.

[9 → 1]   [21 → 13]   [49 → ?]

A 52   **B** 47   **C** 39   **D** 20   **E** 41

16.

[21 → 3]   [42 → 6]   [28 → ?]

A 12   **B** 12   **C** 4   **D** 8   **E** 32

17.

[48 → 6]   [32 → 4]   [8 → ?]

A 6   **B** 12   **C** 30   **D** 1   **E** 24

18.

×3
−1

×3
−1

[11 → 32]   [2 → 5]   [6 → ?]

A 10   **B** 17   **C** 18   **D** 20   **E** 11

$7^2 = 7 \times 7 = 49$

Number Series

$6^2 = 6 \times 6 = 36$

1.

| **1** | **3** | **5** | **7** | **?** |

A 1   **B** 9   **C** 11   **D** 7   **E** 19

$4^2 = 4 \times 2 = 8$ $4 \times 4 = 16$

$5^2 = 5 \times 5 = 25$

2.

| **5** | **3** | **5** | **3** | **5** | **?** |

A 1   **B** 12   **C** 3   **D** 7   **E** 11

$\frac{1}{2}$ $2^2 =$ 2^3 $2^{(4)}$ 2^5

2   2×2 $2 \times 2 \times 2$ $2 \times 2 \times 2 \times 2$ $2 \times 2 \times 2 \times 2 \times 2$

3.

| **2** | **4** | **8** | **16** | **32** | **?** |

A 50   **B** 100   **C** 12   **D** 48   **E** 64 2^6

$3^2 = 9 \quad 3 \times 3 = 9$

$3^3 = 3 \times 3 \times 3 = 27 \quad 2^2 = 2 \times 2 = 4$

4.

| **2** | **4** | **6** | **3** | **5** | **7** | **4** | **?** |

A 4   **B** 21   **C** 6   **D** 12   **E** 1

5.

2   9   15   20   ?

A 24   **B** 9   **C** 12   **D** 23   **E** 18

6.

−1 +4 −1 +4 −1 +4

1   0   4   3   7   6   ?

A 2   **B** 10   **C** 7   **D** 6   **E** 9

7.

5   0   5   0   5   ?

A 0   **B** 2   **C** 5   **D** 12   **E** 4

8.

−4 +2 −4 +2 −4 +2

11   7   9   5   7   3   ?

A 9   **B** 11   **C** 1   **D** 5   **E** 2

9.

-6 -6 -6 -6 -6

42   **36**   **30**   **24**   **18**   **?**

A 8   **B** 5   **C** 30   **(D)** 12   **E** 2

10.

$+5$ -4 $+5$ -4 $+5$ -4

2   **7**   **3**   **8**   **4**   **9**   **?**

(A) 5   **B** 2   **C** 21   **D** 6   **E** 12

11.

$+11$ $+11$ $+11$ $+11$ $+11$ $+11$

7   **18**   **29**   **40**   **51**   **62**   **?**

A 21   **B** 22   **(C)** 73   **D** 30   **E** 15

12.

$+3$ -4 $+3$ -4 $+3$ -4

4   **7**   **3**   **6**   **2**   **5**   **?**

A 11   **B** 0   **C** 20   **D** 2   **(E)** 1

13.

99   98   88   87   77   76   ?

A 66   **B** 10   **C** 29   **D** 3   **E** 50

14.   +5   +5   +5   +5   +5   +5

0.5   5.5   10.5   15.5   20.5   25.5   ?

A 0.1   **B** 6.5   **C** 0.35   **D** 4.5   **E** 30,5

15.

0.11   0.20   0.29   0.38   0.47   ?

A 0.02   **B** 0.1   **C** 0.48   **D** 0.56   **E** 0.9

16.   +1,5   +1,5   +1,5   +1,5   +1,5   +1,5

7   8.5   10   11.5   13   14.5   ?

A 13.5   **B** 7.5   **C** 16   **D** 12   **E** 15.5

17.

$+14$ $+14$ $+14$ $+14$ $+14$ $+14$

41   **55**   **69**   **83**   **97**   **111**   **?**

A 68   **B** 125   **C** 121   **D** 95   **E** 73

18.

$+3.5$ $+3.5$ $+3.5$

2   **5.5**   **9**   **12.5**   **16**   **19.5**   **?**

A 12.5   **B** 1.5   **C** 1,5   **D** 23   **E** 25

ANSWER KEY FOR PRACTICE TEST 1 GRADE 3

Verbal Analogies Practice Test 1 Grade 3
p.17

1.
Answer: option D
Explanation: black is the color of the coal; white is the color of the snow.

2.
Answer: option A
Explanation: the glove contains the hand; the shoe contains the foot.

3.
Answer: option C
Explanation: birds are in the sky; fishes are in the sea.

4.
Answer: option D
Explanation: the opposite of left is right; the opposite of horizontal is vertical.

5.
Answer: option A
Explanation: "many" indicates a large number of things; "few" indicates a small number of things.

6.
Answer: option D
Explanation: hip suggests the first joint leading to the foot (ankle) as shoulder suggests the first joint leading to the hand (wrist).

7.
Answer: option B
Explanation: the superlative degree of warm is hot. Similarly, the superlative degree of old is antique.

8.
Answer: option D

Explanation: the opposite of evening is morning; the opposite of dinner is breakfast.

9.
Answer: option B

Explanation: butcher uses the knife; hairdresser uses the scissors

10.
Answer: option C

Explanation: the bow throws an arrow; the gun throws a bullet

11.
Answer: option B

Explanation: child is a young human; poult is a young bird.

12.
Answer: option C

Explanation: the house of a bee is a hive; the house of a bear is a den.

13.
Answer: option B

Explanation: bacteria cause decomposition; yeasts cause fermentation.

14.
Answer: option A

Explanation: palate is the roof of the mouth; ceiling is the roof of the room.

15.
Answer: option B

Explanation: bridge is built to cross a river. Similarly, tunnels are created to cross the mountains.

16.
Answer: option B
Explanation: students have to pass the exam before being promoted to the next class. Similarly, employees have to undergo appraisal before getting a promotion or increment.

17.
Answer: option B
Explanation: the job of a doctor is to treat patients. Similarly, the job of a teacher is to teach students.

18.
Answer: option A
Explanation: the words implausible and absurd have the same meaning, but implausible is used in a positive sense, whereas absurd is used in a negative sense. The words surprising and shocking mean the same, but surprising is used in a positive sense, shocking is used in a negative sense.

19.
Answer: option C
Explanation: after is the opposite of before, successor is the opposite of predecessor.

20.
Answer: option D
Explanation: sedatives are used to reduce pain; consolation reduces the grief.

21.
Answer: option C
Explanation: an archipelago is a group of islands; a constellation is a group of stars.

22.
Answer: option D
Explanation: France is a state of Europe; Canada is a State of North America.

Verbal Classification Practice Test 1 Grade 3
p.24

1.
Answer: option C
Explanation: leopard, cougar and lion are felines; cat is a feline.

2.
Answer: option B
Explanation: couch, table, and chair are pieces of furniture; bed is also a piece of furniture.

3.
Answer: option C
Explanation: pupil, cornea and retina are parts of the eye; iris is also a part of the eye.

4.
Answer: option B
Explanation: branch, leaf and root are all parts of a tree; bark is also a part of a tree.

5.
Answer: option B
Explanation: index, glossary and chapter are all parts of a book; bibliography is also a part of a book.

6.
Answer: option A
Explanation: unimportant, trivial, insignificant, trifling are synonyms.

7.
Answer: option B
Explanation: core, seeds, and pulp are all parts of an apple; skin is also a part of an apple.

8.

Answer: option D

Explanation: peninsula, island and cape are all landforms; cliff is also a landform.

9.

Answer: option C

Explanation: biology, chemistry, and zoology are all branches of science; astronomy is also a branch of science.

10.

Answer: option A

Explanation: evaluate, assess, appraise and estimate are all synonyms.

11.

Answer: option A

Explanation: water, tea, gasoline are liquid; milk is also liquid.

12.

Answer: option B

Explanation: seagull, swallow and eagle are classified as birds in zoological terms; penguin is also classified as bird in zoological terms.

13.

Answer: option C

Explanation: dog, monkey and lion are mammals; dolphin is also a mammal.

14.

Answer: option A

Explanation: Atlantic, Indian, Pacific are Oceans; Arctic is also an Ocean.

15.

Answer: option C

Explanation: snake, crocodile and lizard are part of a group of animals known as reptiles; turtle is also a reptile.

16.
Answer: option A
Explanation: car, truck and bike have wheels; tractor has wheels.

17.
Answer: option E
Explanation: Chinese, Arabian and Italian are languages; Spanish is also a language.

18.
Answer: option B
Explanation: triangle, square, circle are plane figures; pentagon is also a plan figure.

19.
Answer: option C
Explanation: seeing, hearing, smelling and tasting are actions of five senses.

20.
Answer: option A
Explanation: broccoli, lettuce, tomato are vegetables; carrot is also a vegetable.

Sentence Completion Practice Test 1 grade 3 p.30

1.
Answer: option C
Explanation: blonde hair and beautiful skin suggest a young woman.

2.
Answer: option A
Explanation: short legs suggest a little dog.

3.
Answer: option D
Explanation: a school field trip needs to be organized.

4.
Answer: option C
Explanation: seldom = not often.

5.
Answer: option B
Explanation: gobbled = shallowed.

6.
Answer: option C
Explanation: bright = luminous.

7.
Answer: option D
Explanation: the wedding suggests a strong emotion.

8.
Answer: option C
Explanation: safe = not dangerous.

9.
Answer: option B
Explanation: adequate = the right amount.

10.
Answer: option E
Explanation: death was a consequence of lack of care.

11.
Answer: option C
Explanation: endorse = approve.

12.
Answer: option A
Explanation: boring = not very interesting.

13.
Answer: option D
Explanation: dismal = unhappy.

14.
Answer: option D
Explanation: minuscule = extremely small.

15.
Answer: option E
Explanation: ancient = very old.

16.
Answer: option C
Explanation: unethical = morally unacceptable.

17.
Answer: option D
Explanation: enemies = who try to harm each other.

18.
Answer: option E
Explanation: amazing = surprising.

19.
Answer: option C
Explanation: predict = to say that something will happen, before it happens.

20.
Answer: option E
Explanation: competition = situation in which people or organizations attempt to be more successful than other people or organizations.

Figure Matrices Practice Test 1 Grade 3
p.39

1.
Answer: option A
Explanation: white becomes black; black becomes white.

2.
Answer: option C
Explanation: white, white, black; black, white, white; same shapes.

3.
Answer: option D
Explanation: a black circle over a white shape pointing up becomes a white circle under a white shape pointing down.

4.
Answer: option B
Explanation: white arrow becomes black; black background becomes white.

5.
Answer: option A
Explanation: five-pointed star: pentagon (five-sided) = four-pointed star: square (four-sided).

6.
Answer: option E
Explanation: (pentagon in square: hexagon in pentagon) = (square in triangle: pentagon in square). Larger shapes have 1 less side than the smaller inside shapes. The shapes on the right have one more side than the figures on the left.

7.
Answer: option C
Explanation: (black square containing white pentagon: rotated black pentagon) = (black triangle containing white triangle: rotated black triangle).

8.
Answer: option D
Explanation: (square containing pentagon: pentagon) = (triangle containing triangle: triangle).

9.
Answer: option B
Explanation: same concentric shapes with the addition of a black dot.

10.
Answer: option A
Explanation: (pentagon in a grey square: grey square) = (star in a black triangle: black triangle).The inside shape is removed.

11.
Answer: option B
Explanation: addition of a star above the left shapes.

12.
Answer: option C
Explanation: half width without diagonals.

13.
Answer: option D
Explanation: (two arrows pointing right on a square: two arrows pointing up on a square) = (one arrow pointing right on a square: one arrow pointing up on a square).

14.
Answer: option A
Explanation: (two lines on a grey square: one line on a grey square) = (four lines on a grey square: three lines on a grey square); (one less).

15.

Answer: option B

Explanation: (four parts of a circle with two hearts: two parts of a circle with one heart) = (four parts of a square with two hearts: two parts of a square with one heart).

16.

Answer: option E

Explanation: (four: four) = (three: three).

17.

Answer: option C

Explanation: (three stars: three circles) = (two stars: two circles).

18.

Answer: option E

Explanation: one less black triangle.

19.

Answer: option A

Explanation: (arrow over triangle, triangle over circle): (arrow in triangle, triangle in circle) = (arrow over heart, heart over square): (arrow in heart, heart in square). Combos of same shapes.

20.

Answer: option C

Explanation: the shape within moves to the right.

Figure Classification Practice Test 1 Grade 3
p.47

1.
Answer: option C.
Explanation: same shapes, the smaller one inside the larger one (heptagon within heptagon).

2.
Answer: option C
Explanation: each figure is divided into two halves by a vertical line.

3.
Answer: option C
Explanation: rhombus above larger rhombus, pentagon above larger pentagon, circle above larger circle, hexagon above larger hexagon.

4.
Answer: option D
Explanation: 1 vertical line and 1 horizontal line inside each shape.

5.
Answer: option D
Explanation: four-sided shapes.

6.
Answer: option C
Explanation: four lines in each shape.

7.

Answer: option A

Explanation: pentagon is a five-sided polygon; star is a ten-sided shape (double). Square is a four-sided polygon; octagon is an eight-sided polygon (double). Triangle is a three-sided polygon; hexagon is a six-sided polygon (double). Hexagon is a six-sided polygon; cross shape is a twelve-sided shape (double).

8.

Answer: option A

Explanation: twelve-sided shapes.

9.

Answer: option B

Explanation: combos of triangle, circle, square.

10.

Answer: option E

Explanation: two grey circles lie on the opposite sides of a diagonal.

11.

Answer: option E

Explanation: the arrows intersect each other at right angle.

12.

Answer: option D

Explanation: four shapes in each square, each one with a different orientation.

13.

Answer: option C

Explanation: rectangle and circle are across from another.

14.

Answer: option A

Explanation: arrows pointing right.

15.

Answer: option B

Explanation: rounded shapes.

16.

Answer: option D

Explanation: single straight line at same point on figure.

17.

Answer: option E

Explanation: figures of same size.

18.

Answer: option A

Explanation: squares divided into equal parts.

19.

Answer: option C

Explanation: circle and star next to each other.

20.

Answer: option C

Explanation: circles with lines from upper right to lower left.

Paper Folding Practice Test 1 Grade 3
p.58

1.
Answer: option A

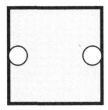

2.
Answer: option A

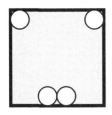

3.
Answer: option B

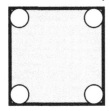

4.
Answer: option A

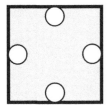

5.
Answer: option A

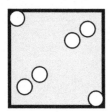

6.
Answer: option C

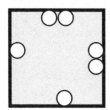

7
Answer: option D

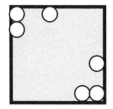

8.
Answer: option A

9.
Answer: option B

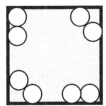

10.
Answer: option A

11.
Answer: option C

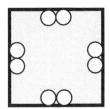

12.
Answer: option B

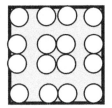

13.
Answer: option A

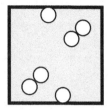

14.
Answer: option D

15.
Answer: option E

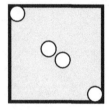

16.
Answer: option A

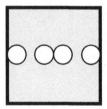

Number Puzzle Practice Test 1 Grade 3
p.69

1.
Answer: option A
Explanation: 10-6=4; 4=4

2.
Answer: option C
Explanation: 5+5=10; 10=10

3.
Answer: option B
Explanation: 4+2=6; 6=6

4.
Answer: option C
Explanation: 2X3=5+1; 6=6

5.
Answer: option E
Explanation: 13-3=9+1; 10=10

6.
Answer: option B
Explanation: 20+12=45-13; 32=32

7.
Answer: option A
Explanation: 90=100-3-7; 90=90

8.
Answer: option E
Explanation: 25=50-27+2; 25=23+2; 25=25

9.
Answer: option D
Explanation: 88=25+43+20; 88=68+20; 88=88

10.
Answer: option D
Explanation: 78-21=89-32; 57=57

11.
Answer: option A
Explanation: 23+19=45-3; 42=42

12.
Answer: option B
Explanation: 64-18 =98-52; 46=46

13.
Answer: option E
Explanation: 71=25+46; 71=71

14.
Answer: option C
Explanation: 35=7X5; 35=35

15.
Answer: option B
Explanation: 56=8X7; 56=56

16.
Answer: option C
Explanation: ◆ = 13+4; ◆ =17; 24=17+7

Number Analogies Practice Test 1 Grade 3
p.75

1.
Answer: option B
Explanation: 9+3=12   5+3=8   15+3=18

2.
Answer: option A
Explanation: 5X2=10   8X2=16   3X2=6

3.
Answer: option B
Explanation: 13-3=10   8-3=5   15-3=12

4.
Answer: option D
Explanation: 10:2=5   8:2=4   18:2=9

5.
Answer: option E
Explanation: 5+5=10; 10+2=12   3+3=6; 6+2=8   11+11=22; 22+2=24

6.
Answer: option A
Explanation: 5X8=40   8X8=64   3X8=24

7.
Answer: option C
Explanation: 5X3=15; 15-1=14   1X3=3; 3-1=2   3X3=9; 9-1=8

8.
Answer: option D
Explanation: 20-9=11   35-9=26   11-9=2

9.
Answer: option A
Explanation: 15-7=8   30-7=23   11-7=4

10.
Answer: option E
Explanation: 23+4=27   31+4=35   25+4=29

11.
Answer: option C
Explanation: 20+4=24   35+4=39   11+4=15

12.
Answer: option A
Explanation: 8X5=40   2X5=10   10X5=50

13.
Answer: option D
Explanation: 18:3=6   36:3=12   6:3=2

14.
Answer: option C
Explanation: 20-12=8   35-12=23   19-12=7

15.
Answer: option B
Explanation: 9-3=6   22-3=19   50-3=47

16.
Answer: option D
Explanation: 28:7=4   35:7=5   63:7=9

17.
Answer: option A
Explanation: 24:8=3   32:8=4   8:8=1

18.
Answer: option B
Explanation: 20X2=40; 40-2=38   35X2=70; 70-2=68
11X2=22; 22-2=20

Number Series Practice Test 1 Grade 3
p.81

1.
Answer: option A
Explanation: +4, +4, +4, +4, etc. 2+4=6; 6+4=10; 10+4=14: 14+4=18

2.
Answer: option C
Explanation: -1, -1, -1, -1, -1, etc.

3.
Answer: option E
Explanation: +6, -3, +6, -3, +6, etc.

4.
Answer: option B
Explanation: +5, -4, +5, -4, +5, -4, +5, etc.

5.
Answer: option E
Explanation: +5, +4, +3, +2, etc.

6.
Answer: option C
Explanation: -1, +3, -1, +3, -1, +3, etc.

7.
Answer: option E
Explanation: -3, +3, -3, +3, -3, etc.

8.
Answer: option C
Explanation: -3, +1, -3, +1, -3, +1, etc.

9.
Answer: option A
Explanation: -5, -5, -5, -5, -5, etc.

10.
Answer: option E
Explanation: +1, +2, +1, +2, +1, +2, etc.

11.
Answer: option B
Explanation: +2, +5, +2, +5, +2, +5, etc.

12.
Answer: option B
Explanation: +3, -4, +3, -4, +3, -4, etc.

13.
Answer: option E
Explanation: +3, +0, +3, +0, +3, +0, etc.

14.
Answer: option B
Explanation: +1, +1, +1, +1, +1, +1, etc.

15.
Answer: option D
Explanation: +0.05, +0.05, +0.05, +0.05, +0.05, +0.05, etc.

16.
Answer: option A
Explanation: -11, -11, -11, -11, -11, -11, etc.

17.
Answer: option D
Explanation: +9, +9, +9, +9, +9, +9, etc.

18.
Answer: option A
Explanation: +1.5, +1.5, +1.5, +1.5, +1.5, +1.5, etc.

ANSWER KEY FOR PRACTICE TEST 2 GRADE 3

Verbal Analogies Practice Test 2 Grade 3
p.88

1.
Answer: option C
Explanation: yellow is the color of the lemon; red is the color of the blood.

2.
Answer: option B
Explanation: a watch is worn on the wrist; a chain is worn on the neck.

3.
Answer: option A
Explanation: earthquake causes tsunami; heavy rain causes flood.

4.
Answer: option D
Explanation: sunrise is the time when the sun first appears in the morning; dawn is the time at the beginning of the day, when light first appears. Sunset is the time of day when the sun disappears and night begins; dusk is the time before it gets dark, when the sky is becoming less bright.

5.
Answer: option C
Explanation: dwarf is an imaginary creature that looks like a small man; giant is a big man.

6.
Answer: option D
Explanation: a cooked food is hot; a cold food is refrigerated.

7.
Answer: option B
Explanation: pinch causes pain; hug causes comfort.

8.
Answer: option B
Explanation: sniff is to breathe air into your nose; lick is to move your tongue across the surface of something in order to eat it.

9.
Answer: option E
Explanation: tired: feeling that you want to sleep or rest. Hungry: wanting to eat something.

10.
Answer: option B
Explanation: singer is a person who sings; orator is a public speaker.

11.
Answer: option B
Explanation: opposites.

12.
Answer: option B
Explanation: plane moves through the air; ship moves in the water.

13.
Answer: option C
Explanation: opposites.

14.
Answer: option B
Explanation: chapters are a part of a book just as a fender is a part of an automobile.

15.
Answer: option C
Explanation: mirrors are smooth just as sandpaper is rough.

16.

Answer: option A

Explanation: the function of a knife is to cut. The function of a shovel is to dig.

17.

Answer: option D

Explanation: a fish can be found in the sea, just as a moose can be found in a forest.

18.

Answer: option B

Explanation: these words differ in degree. One is more intense than the other is.

19.

Answer: option B

Explanation: a carpenter works with wood, just as a plumber works with pipes.

20.

Answer: option C

Explanation: an author writes just as a chef cooks.

21.

Answer: option A

Explanation: zoologists study animals; botanists study plants.

22.

Answer: option B

Explanation: sculptor is an artist who creates statues; a poet is an artist who writes poems.

Verbal Classification Practice Test 2 Grade 3
p.94

1.
Answer: option D
Explanation: man, monkey, macaque and lemur are Primates.

2.
Answer: option A
Explanation: copper, zinc, aluminum, bronze are metals.

3.
Answer: option E
Explanation: eye, nose, mouth and ears are on the head.

4.
Answer: option C
Explanation: beak, wing, tail, feathers are parts of a bird.

5.
Answer: option E
Explanation: parrot, bat, crow and eagle are flying animals.

6.
Answer: option D
Explanation: Italy, Spain, France and Greece are in Europe.

7.
Answer: option D
Explanation: allow, permit, let and consent are synonyms.

8.
Answer: option C
Explanation: snow, rain, hail and sleet are particles falling from clouds.

9.
Answer: option A

Explanation: beat, hit, strike and knock are synonyms.

10.
Answer: option B

Explanation: brave, courageous, valiant and heroic are all synonyms.

11.
Answer: option E

Explanation: parallelogram, rectangle, square and rhombus are all four-sided polygons.

12.
Answer: option C

Explanation: incorporate, comprise, include and contain are all synonyms.

13.
Answer: option E

Explanation: shark, trout, salmon and blue marlin are fishes.

14.
Answer: option B

Explanation: Mediterranean, Caribbean, Caspian and Baltic are Seas.

15.
Answer: option D

Explanation: bees, fly, ant and butterfly are insects.

16.
Answer: option A

Explanation: elephant, goat, gazelle and cow are herbivores.

17.
Answer: option B
Explanation: lamp, candle, fire and Sun make light.

18.
Answer: option C
Explanation: demand, claim, require, and need are synonyms.

19.
Answer: option D
Explanation: door, window, balcony and roof are parts of a house.

20.
Answer: option C
Explanation: fulfill, realize, accomplish and reach are synonyms.

Sentence Completion Practice Test 2 Grade 3
p.99

1.
Answer: option C
Explanation: long black hair and green eyes suggest a beautiful woman.

2.
Answer: option A
Explanation: massive = very big

3.
Answer: option B
Explanation: calculate = determining how long the distance is.

4.
Answer: option B
Explanation: always = all the time, at all times, or every time

5.
Answer: option D
Explanation: collected = in control of thoughts, feelings etc.

6.
Answer: option B
Explanation: wet = covered in water or another liquid.

Answer: option B
Explanation: tired = to feel very annoyed and bored with something that has continued for too long.

8.
Answer: option A
Explanation: toxic = containing poison.

9.
Answer: option E
Explanation: insufficient = not enough

10.
Answer: option E
Explanation: rejected = to refuse to accept an idea.

11.
Answer: option E
Explanation: refuse = to say firmly that you will not do something.

12.
Answer: option C
Explanation: modern = belonging to the present time or most recent time.

13.
Answer: option E
Explanation: standard = the level that is considered to be acceptable.

14.
Answer: option E
Explanation: monumental = very important.

15.
Answer: option C
Explanation: immense = extremely large.

16.
Answer: option A
Explanation: genuine = a genuine feeling is one that you really feel, not one you pretend to feel.

17.
Answer: option C
Explanation: companions = someone you spend a lot of time with, especially a friend.

18.
Answer: option A
Explanation: huge = extremely large.

19.
Answer: option B
Explanation: fallen = the past participle of fall.

20.
Answer: option C
Explanation: confidence = the feeling that you can trust someone.

Figure Matrices Practice Test 2 Grade 3
p.106

1.
Answer: option C
Explanation: same shapes but in opposite positions.

2.
Answer: option D
Explanation: the lower shape moves to the right.

3.
Answer: option B
Explanation: the upper shape becomes the lower.

4.
Answer: option E
Explanation: smaller shape becomes black; background becomes white.

5.
Answer: option D
Explanation: (three-sided shape: four-sided shapes) = (six sided shape: seven-sided shape) (one more).

6.
Answer: option A
Explanation: (ten-sided shape: five-sided shape) = (eight-sided shape: four-sided shape) (half).

7.
Answer: option E
Explanation: the smaller interior shape is removed.

8.

Answer: option C

Explanation: (four circles: two circles) = (two circles: one circle) (half).

9.

Answer: option B

Explanation: (one square with a black circle: two squares with a black circle) = (one hexagon with a black circle: two hexagons with a black circle).

10.

Answer: option A

Explanation: the larger shape is removed.

11.

Answer: option C

Explanation: (black star in a white triangle): (black triangle in a white star) = (black circle in a white arrow): (black arrow in a white circle).

12.

Answer: option A

Explanation: diagonals elimination.

13.

Answer: option E

Explanation: (one black arrow pointing up on a square: one black arrow pointing down on a square) = (one arrow pointing right on a square: one arrow pointing left on a square). Opposites.

14.

Answer: option E

Explanation: smaller shape is removed.

15.

Answer: option B

Explanation: one less diagonal, two more hearts.

16.
Answer: option D
Explanation: (four: four) = (two: two).

17.
Answer: option C
Explanation: elimination of black and grey circles.

18.
Answer: option B
Explanation: elimination of one black triangle and one grey triangle.

19.
Answer: Option D
Explanation: elimination of the lower shape.

20.
Answer: option A
Explanation: (twelve-sided shapes: ten sided shape) = (ten-sided shape: eight-sided shape). Two sides less.

Figure Classification Practice Test 2 Grade 3
p.113

1.
Answer: option E
Explanation: three equal shapes, one inside the other.

2.
Answer: option C
Explanation: each figure is divided into two sections by a horizontal line.

3.
Answer: option E
Explanation: four-sided shapes.

4.
Answer: option B
Explanation: four lines in a shape.

5.
Answer: option D
Explanation: a triangle in a four-sided shape.

6.
Answer: option E
Explanation: seven-sided shapes in seven-sided shapes.

7.
Answer: option A
Explanation: larger shape has 1 more side than the smaller inside shape.

8.

Answer: option B

Explanation: grey circle within a 12-sided shape.

9.

Answer: option B

Explanation: combos of triangle, square, black arrow.

10.

Answer: option E

Explanation: the grey circle lies on one side of the diagonal. On the other side, there are two black circles.

11.

Answer: option D

Explanation: arrows point to right.

12.

Answer: option B

Explanation: two grey shapes, one on the right and one on the left.

13.

Answer: option C

Explanation: two four-sided shapes in a square.

14.

Answer: option D

Explanation: arrows pointing down.

15.

Answer: option D

Explanation: combos of triangle, grey heart and circle.

16.
Answer: option D
Explanation: three down arrows; one up arrow.

17.
Answer: option A
Explanation: seven-sided shapes.

18.
Answer: option C
Explanation: ten-sided shapes in a square.

19.
Answer: option C
Explanation: four squares, a grey star, a circle and a heart

20.
Answer: option B
Explanation: two concentric circles, same color.

Paper Folding Practice Test 2 Grade 3
p.123

1.
Answer: Option B

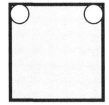

2.
Answer: Option A

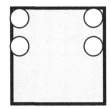

3.
Answer: Option E

4.
Answer: Option C

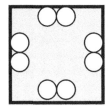

5.
Answer: Option D

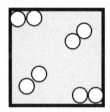

6.
Answer: Option C

7.
Answer: Option D

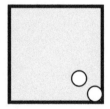

8.
Answer: Option B

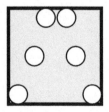

9.

Answer: Option D

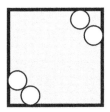

10.

Answer: Option B

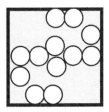

11.

Answer: Option E

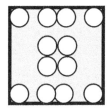

12.

Answer: Option B

13.
Answer: Option A

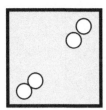

14.
Answer: Option E

15.
Answer: Option C

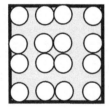

16.
Answer: Option A

Number Puzzle Practice Test 2 Grade 3
p.132

1.
Answer: option A
Explanation: 24-11=13; 13=13

2.
Answer: option B
Explanation: 6+9=15; 15=15

3.
Answer: option E
Explanation: 8+2=10; 10=10

4.
Answer: option B
Explanation: 5X2=9+1; 10=10

5.
Answer: option D
Explanation: 25-3=21+1; 22=22

6.
Answer: option E
Explanation: 33+14=50-3; 47=47

7.
Answer: option A
Explanation: 90=100-3-7; 90=90

8.
Answer: option B
Explanation: 32=51-40+21; 32=11+21; 32=32

9.
Answer: option A
Explanation: 66=12+27+27; 66=66

10.
Answer: option B
Explanation: 92-33=61-2; 59=59

11.
Answer: option A
Explanation: 29+17=62-16; 46=46

12.
Answer: option C
Explanation: 78-9 =92-23; 69=69

13.
Answer: option C
Explanation: 22=10+12; 22=22

14.
Answer: option E
Explanation: 63=9X7; 63=63

15.
Answer: option A
Explanation: 42=2X21; 42=42

16.
Answer: option D
Explanation: 5=6-1;   35=6+29;   35=35

Number Analogies Practice Test 2 Grade 3
p.137

1.
Answer: option A
Explanation: 9+5=14   5+5=10   15+5=20

2.
Answer: option C
Explanation: 4X2=8   8X2=16   14X2=28

3.
Answer: option E
Explanation: 10-3=7   6-3=3   12-3=9

4.
Answer: option C
Explanation: 6:3=2   12:3=4   18:3=6

5.
Answer: option D
Explanation: 5+6=11   3+6=9   11+6=17

6.
Answer: option A
Explanation: 6X7=42   8X7=56   3X7=21

7.
Answer: option C
Explanation: 6X3=18; 18-1=17   1X3=3; 3-1=2   4X3=12;   12-1=11

8.
Answer: option D
Explanation: 20-7=13   35-7=28   50-7=43

9.
Answer: option A
Explanation: 19-11=8   30-11=19   11-11=0

10.
Answer: option E
Explanation: 19+4=23   29+4=33   21+4=25

11.
Answer: option B
Explanation: 21+6=27   32+6=38   11+6=17

12.
Answer: option A
Explanation: 7X5=35   3X5=15   20X5=100

13.
Answer: option C
Explanation: 15:3=5   33:3=11   9:3=3

14.
Answer: option A
Explanation: 22-12=10   34-12=22   13-12=1

15.
Answer: option E
Explanation: 9-8=1   21-8=13   49-8=41

16.
Answer: option C
Explanation: 21:7=3   42:7=6   28:7=4

17.
Answer: option D
Explanation: 48:8=6   32:8=4   8:8=1

18.
Answer: option B
Explanation: 11X3=33; 33-1=32   2X3=6; 6-1=5   6X3=18; 18-1=17

Number Series Practice Test 2 Grade 3
p.142

1.
Answer: option B
Explanation: +2. +2, +2, +2, etc.

2.
Answer: option C
Explanation: -2, +2, -2, +2, -2 etc.

3.
Answer: option E
Explanation: x2, x2, x2, x2, x2 etc.

4.
Answer: option C
Explanation: +2, +2, -3, +2, +2, -3, +2, etc.

5.
Answer: option A
Explanation: +7, +6, +5, +4, etc.

6.
Answer: option B
Explanation: -1, +4, -1, +4, -1, +4, etc.

7.
Answer: option A
Explanation: -5, +5, -5, +5, -5, etc.

8.
Answer: option D
Explanation: -4, +2, -4, +2, -4, +2, etc.

9.
Answer: option D
Explanation: -6, -6, -6, -6, -6, etc.

10.
Answer: option A
Explanation: +5, -4, +5, -4, +5, -4, etc.

11.
Answer: option C
Explanation: +11, +11, +11, +11, +11, +11, etc.

12.
Answer: option E
Explanation: +3, -4, +3, -4, +3, -4, etc.

13.
Answer: option A
Explanation: -1, -10, -1, -10, -1, -10, etc.

14.
Answer: option E
Explanation: +5, +5, +5, +5, +5, +5, etc.

15.
Answer: option D
Explanation: +0.09, +0.09, +0.09, +0.09, +0.09, +0.09, etc.

16.
Answer: option C
Explanation: +1.5, +1.5, +1.5, +1.5, +1.5, +1.5, etc.

17.
Answer: option B
Explanation: every number increases by 14.

18.
Answer: option D
Explanation: every number increases by 3.5.

HOW TO DOWNLOAD 54 BONUS QUESTIONS

Thank you for reading this book, we hope you really enjoyed it and found it very helpful.

PLEASE LEAVE US A REVIEW ON THE WEBSITE WHERE YOU PURCHASED THIS BOOK!

By leaving a review, you give us the opportunity to improve our work.

A GIFT FOR YOU!

FREE ONLINE ACCESS TO 54 BONUS PRACTICE QUESTIONS.

Follow this link:

https://www.skilledchildren.com/free-download-cogat-practice-test.php

You will find a PDF to download: please insert this PASSWORD: 17072000

Nicole Howard and The SkilledChildren.com Team

www.skilledchildren.com

COGAT®TEST PREP
GRADE 4

VERBAL BATTERY GRADE 4

This section is designed to assess a student's vocabulary, ability to solve problems associated with vocabulary, ability to determine word relationship and memory retention.

Verbal Analogies

A verbal analogy traces a similarity between a pair of words and another pair of words.

Example

aloof $\longrightarrow$ connected : deliberate $\longrightarrow$

A accidental   **B** new   **C** wanted   **D** known   **E** old

- First, identify the relationship between the first pair of words.
- How do the words "aloof" and "connected" go together?

The opposite of aloof is connected.

- Now, look at the word "deliberate".
- Which of the possible choices follows the previous rule?

The opposite of "deliberate" is "accidental", so the correct answer is A.

Tips for Solving Verbal Analogies

- Try to identify the correlation between the first two words.
- Review all answers before you make a choice.
- Remove any word in the answers that don't have a comparable kind of relationship.
- Also, evaluate the possible alternative meanings of the words.

1.
light → blind : speech →

A clever   **B** awake   **C** deaf   **D** alive
E dumb

2.
distance → meter: liquid →

A kilometer   **B** height   **C** liter   **D** centimeter
E miles

3.
stomachache → stomach : conjunctivitis →

A eye   **B** heart   **C** arm   **D** head   **E** hand

4.
iron → metal : quartz →

A fiber   **B** mineral   **C** wood   **D** leather
E ceramic

5.

fork→ eat : car →

A sing **B** sleep **C** walk **D** travel **E** fly

6.

finger→hand : pupil →

A head **B** bone **C** knee **D** eye **E** leg

7.

rose → flower : pine →

A car **B** tree **C** candy **D** organ **E** instrument

8.

wheel → car : hand →

A sword **B** cat **C** pen **D** bird **E** body

9.

gasoline ⟶ fuel : helium⟶

A metal   **B** gas   **C** stone   **D** balloon   **E** liquid

10.

powerless⟶ efficacy : explicit ⟶

A safety   **B** beauty   **C** ambiguity   **D** clarity
E honestly

11.

wretched ⟶cheerful : innocuous ⟶

A dangerous   **B** safe   **C** new   **D** solitary   **E** old

12.

labyrinth ⟶ complicated : enigma⟶

A easy   **B** mysterious   **C** nice   **D** dark   **E** colorful

13.
neutral ⟶ indifferent : lazy ⟶

A smart **B** indolent **C** nice **D** new **E** clever

14.
avarice ⟶ generosity : jeopardy ⟶

A tenacity **B** revenge **C** nastiness **D** security
E dishonesty

15.
fin ⟶ fish : wing ⟶

A cat **B** hen **C** snake **D** car **E** hand

16.
lion ⟶ strength : cat ⟶

A wickedness **B** agility **C** emaciation
D weakness **E** high

17.

brush→ paint : straw →

A sleep **B** buy **C** swim **D** fly **E** drink

18.

hockey → sport : chemistry →

A science **B** ideology **C** religion **D** joke
E animal

19.

teeth → chew : legs →

A eat **B** walk **C** sing **D** hide **E** pull

20.

selfish → compassion : childish →

A strength **B** intelligence **C** beauty **D** maturity
E youth

21.

doctor → hospital : cashier →

A gym **B** labyrinth **C** supermarket **D** house
E laboratory

22.

sleep → slept : buy →

A food **B** ate **C** eating **D** hungry **E** bought

23.

lenient → strict : punctual →

A ridiculous **B** laggard **C** serious **D** honest
E beautiful

24.

ingredient → recipe : roof →

A body **B** house **C** story **D** book **E** family

Verbal Classification

Verbal classification questions ask the student to choose the voice that belongs to a group of three words.

Example

yellow, green, blue

A nice   **B** brown   **C** hard   **D** new   **E** soft

- First, identify the relationship between the three words in the first row.
- What do the words yellow, green and blue have in common?

Yellow, green, and blue are all colors.

- Now, look at the five worlds: nice, brown, hard, new, and soft. Which word goes best with the three words in the top row?

Brown is also a color, so the correct answer is B.

Tips for Solving Verbal Classification Questions

- Try to identify the correlation between the three words in the top row.
- Review all answers before you make a choice.
- Remove every word in the answers that don't have any kind of relationship with the three words in the top row.
- Also, evaluate the possible alternative meanings of the words.

1.
date, day, month

A calendar   **B** book   **C** library   **D** hour   **E** year

2.
carrot, ginger, lettuce

A apple   **B** orange   **C** celery   **D** pear
E strawberry

3.
Mercury, Venus, Earth

A Mars   **B** Sun   **C** United States   **D** Europe
E Africa

4.
chair, sofa, table

A house   **B** wardrobe   **C** door   **D** roof   **E** wall

5.

sister, brother, father

A friend   **B** colleague   **C** companion   **D** mother
E substitute

6.

lion, cheetah, tiger

A bear   **B** dog   **C** snake   **D** leopard   **E** dolphin

7.

speedboat, sailboat, kayak

A car   **B** yacht   **C** bike   **D** sled   **E** wagon

8.

dragonfly, butterfly, ant

A spider   **B** snake   **C** warm   **D** lizard
E ladybug.

9.

wheat, maize, rye

A celery   **B** quinoa   **C** carrot   **D** potato   **E** onion

10.

Nigeria, Egypt, Ethiopia

A Italy   **B** Albania   **C** Tanzania   **D** Belgium
E Estonia

11.

coke, milk, tea

A juice   **B** bread   **C** oxygen   **D** helium   **E** gas

12.

frog, toad, salamander

A snake   **B** newt   **C** lizard   **D** spider   **E** warm

13.
sea lion, dolphin, whale

A sparrow   **B** cat   **C** porpoise   **D** turtle
E tiger

14.
crocodile, iguana, gecko

A anaconda   **B** warm   **C** spider   **D** giraffe
E eel

15.
akita, beagle, boxer

A cat   **B** lion   **C** bulldog   **D** bear   **E** deer

16.
buy, sell, eat

A create   **B** beauty   **C** apple   **D** pear   **E** bad

17.

Hindi, Japanese, Portuguese

A England   **B** Italy   **C** Brazil   **D** China
E Russian

18.

hexagon, rhombus, octagon

A cube   **B** square   **C** pyramid   **D** cone
E sphere

19.

big, colossal, fat

A attractive   **B** bald   **C** immense   **D** beautiful
E elegant

20.

bedroom, laundry, living room

A kitchen   **B** garden   **C** wall   **D** door   **E** window

Sentence Completion

Complete the phrase using the appropriate word that best fits the meaning of the sentence as a whole.

Example

Drivers should keep a _____ distance from the car in front.

A safe   **B** unsafe   **C** little   **D** amazing   **E** dangerous

- First, read the sentence. You will realize that one word is missing.
- Look at the answer choices under the main sentence. Which word would go better in the phrase?

Safe= not in danger of being harmed. Therefore, the right choice is "A".

Tips for Sentence Completion

- First, read the incomplete phrase.
- Think about what type of word you can use and try to anticipate the answer.
- Remove every word in the answers that don't have any kind of relationship with the main sentence.
- Read the incomplete sentence again.

1.

The turtles lay their eggs in the damp sand where they are _____ from predators.

A unsafe   **B** attracted   **C** safe   **D** discovered
E removed

2.

Psychologists observed that the mice became more aggressive in smaller _____.

A cages   **B** houses   **C** museums   **D** cakes
E circus

3.

To her great _____, she became the mother of two beautiful baby girls.

A pain   **B** sorrow   **C** fear   **D** joy   **E** anger

4.

The whole country experienced a period of _____ after the war ended.

A sadness   **B** depression   **C** euphoria   **D** fear
E immobility

5.

I can still remember the intense excitement of going to _____ my first football match.

A sell   **B** see   **C** remove   **D** avoid   **E** calculate

6.

John spoke of the _____ event in which more than 100 people died.

A beautiful   **B** happy   **C** tragic   **D** exciting
E fantastic

7.

In school, the children also _____ social skills.

A eat   **B** buy   **C** sell   **D** learn   **E** refuse

8.

The order to create wealth can never justify permanent _____ to the balance of nature.

A benefit   **B** health   **C** damage   **D** excitement
E joy

9.

Kim _____ the news without showing any visible sign of emotion.

A bought   **B** received   **C** broke   **D** created
E sold

10.

I bought this CD as a gift for Jane, but she's _____ got it.

A always   **B** never   **C** tomorrow   **D** however
E already

11.

The design of the new house is similar to those that have already been _____.

A killed   **B** held   **C** built   **D** kissed   **E** called

12.

You can visit the desert as part of an _____ 5-day excursion out of the city.

A impressive   **B** bad   **C** boring   **D** useless
E catastrophic

13.

If you buy _____ quality shoes, they last much longer.

A little   **B** dirty   **C** useless   **D** good   **E** bad

14.

Photographs _____ if they are exposed to strong sunlight.

A die   **B** grow   **C** burn   **D** fade   **E** fall

15.

In autumn the leaves _____ lovely colour combinations.

A ruin   **B** enlarge   **C** stain   **D** steal   **E** create

16.

I believe children should _____ music as soon as they are capable of doing so.

A eat   **B** sell   **C** read   **D** publish   **E** move

17.

Medicines should be kept out of the reach of _____.

A man   **B** woman   **C** horse   **D** children
E people

18.

The internet plays a _____ role in disseminating information.

A funny   **B** little   **C** famous   **D** electric   **E** key

19.
Smoking is a major cause of heart _____.

A health   **B** cure   **C** disease   **D** color
E pulse

20.
The boys were suspended from school for _____ behavior.

A good   **B** wonderful   **C** honest   **D** innocent
E bad

NON VERBAL BATTERY GRADE 4

This section is designed to assess a student's ability to reason and think beyond what they've already been taught. This section includes geometric shapes and figures that aren't normally seen in the classroom.

Figure Matrices

Students are provided with a 2X2 matrix with the image missing in one cell. They have to identify the relationship between the two spatial shapes in the upper line and find a fourth image that has the same correlation with the left shape in the lower line.

Example

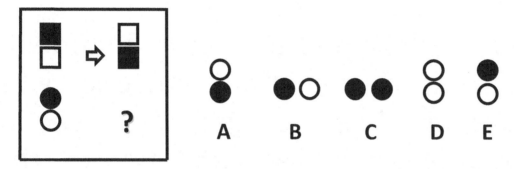

In the upper left box, the image shows a white square and a black square. In the upper right box, the image shows the same squares, but now the white square is above the black square.

The lower left box shows a black circle and a white circle. Which answer choice would go with this image in the same way as the upper images go together?

The image of the answer choice must show two circles but in opposite positions compared to the figures on the left. In other words, the white circle must be above the black circle.
The right answer is "A".

Tips for Figure Matrices

- Consider all the answer choices before selecting one.
- Try to use logic and sequential reasoning.
- Eliminate the logically wrong answers to restrict the options.
- Train yourself to decipher the relationship between different figures and shapes.

1.

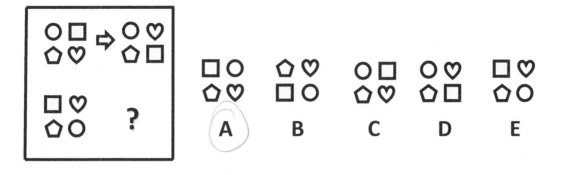

2.

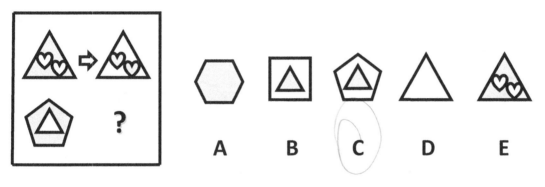

3.

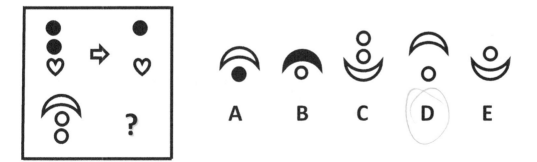

4.

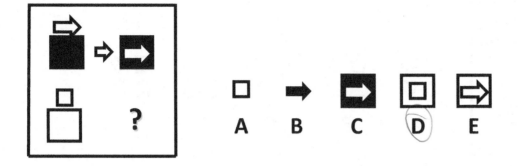

5.

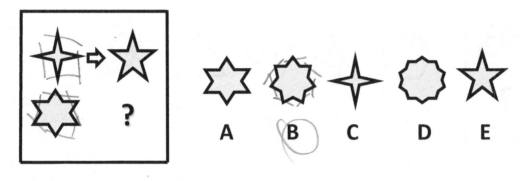

6.

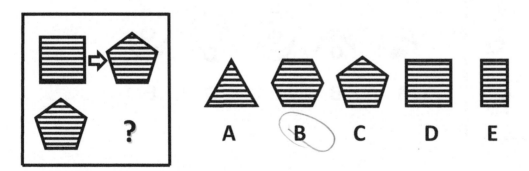

7.

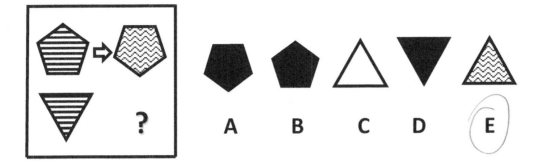

A B C D E

8.

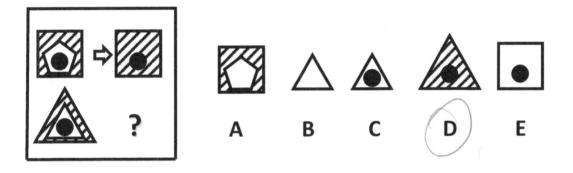

A B C D E

9.

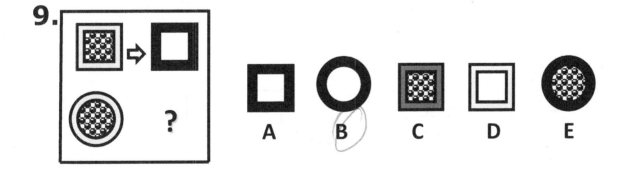

A B C D E

10.

11.

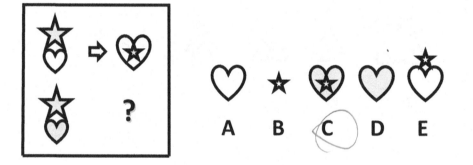

12.

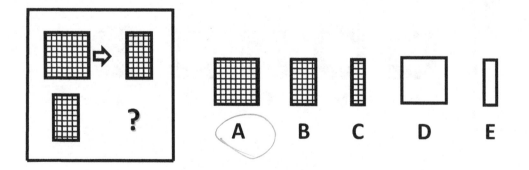

13.

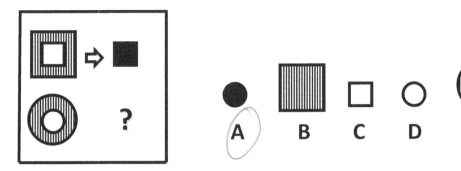

14.

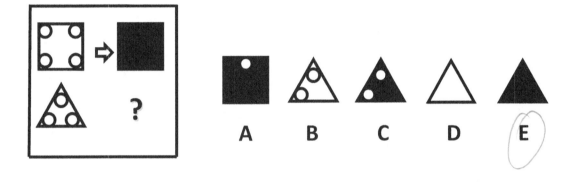

15.

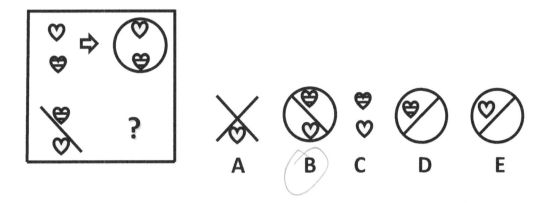

16.

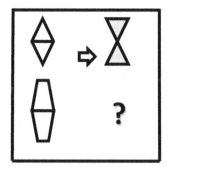 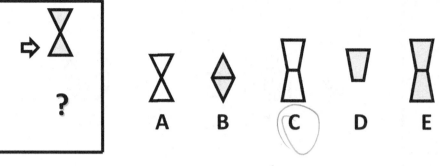

A   **B**   **C**   **D**   **E**

17.

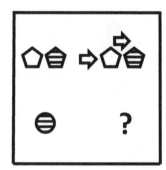 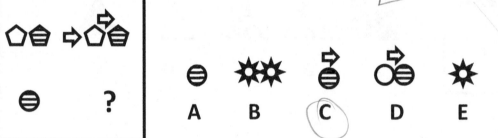

A   **B**   **C**   **D**   **E**

18.

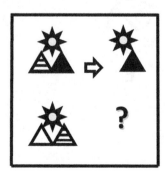 

A   **B**   **C**   **D**   **E**

19.

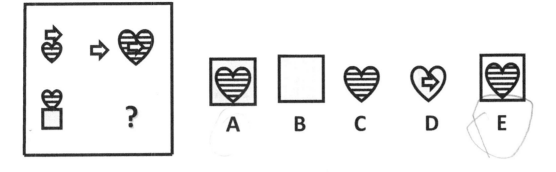

20.

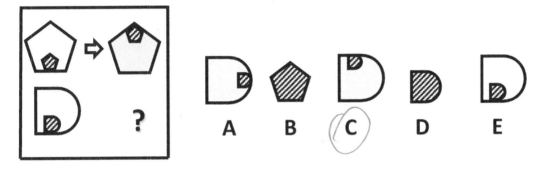

21.

22.

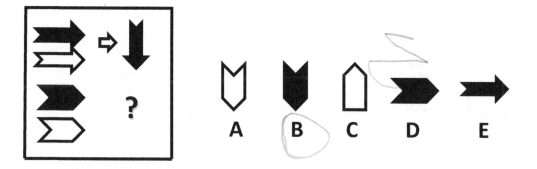

Figure Classification

Students are provided with three shapes and they have to select the answer choice that should be the fourth figure in the set, based on the similarity with the other three figures. The intention is to test the student's ability to recognize similar patterns and to make a rational choice.

Example

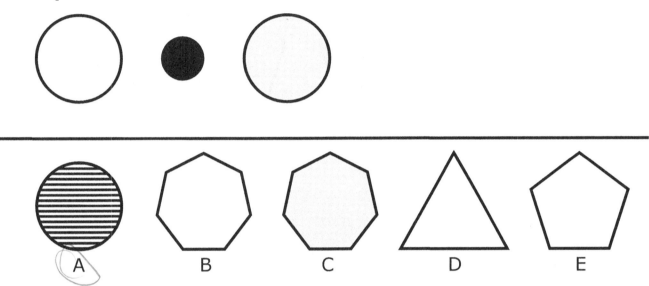

Look at the three pictures on the top. What do these three figures have in common?
You can see three circles in different sizes and colors.
Now, look at the shapes in the row of the answer choices. Which image matches best the three shapes in the top row?

The image of the answer choice must be a circle. The right answer is "A".

Tips for Figure Classification

- Be sure to review all answer choices before selecting one.
- Try to use logic and sequential reasoning.
- Try to exclude the obviously wrong options to reduce the answer choices.

1.

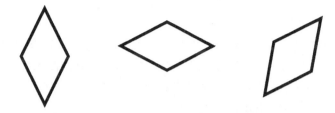

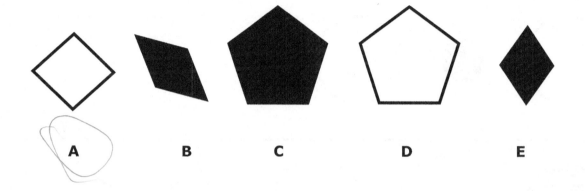

2.

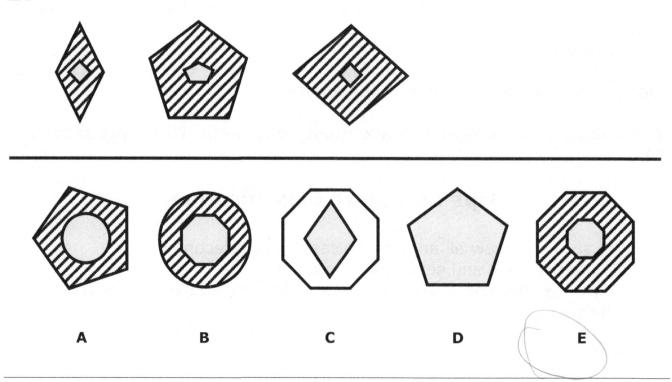

3.

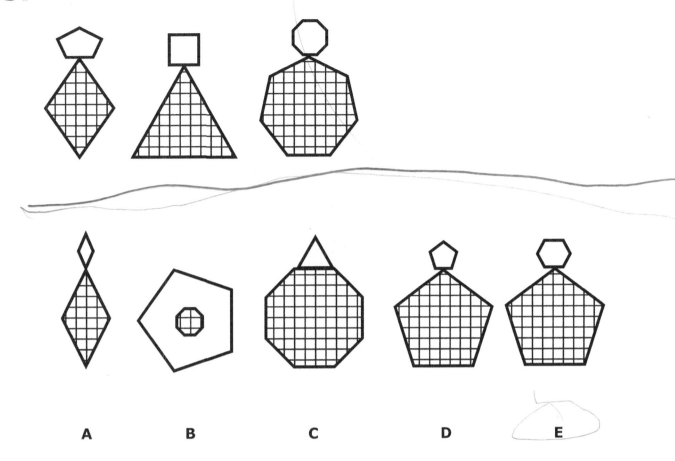

| A | B | C | D | E |

4.

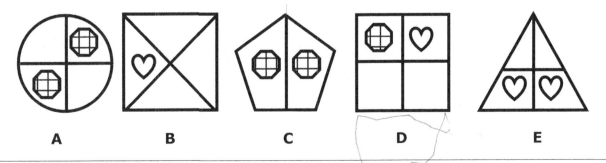

| A | B | C | D | E |

5.

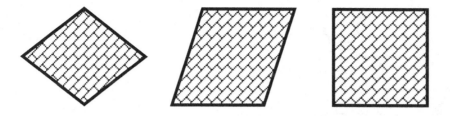

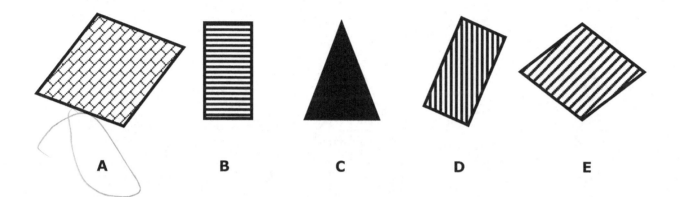

6.

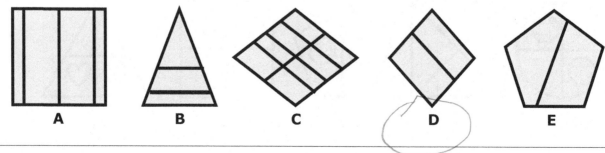

7.

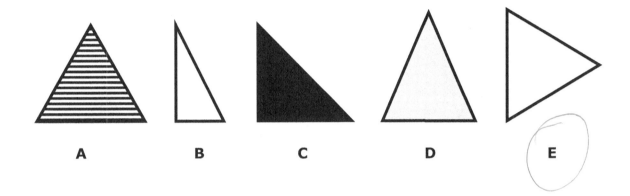

| A | B | C | D | E |

8.

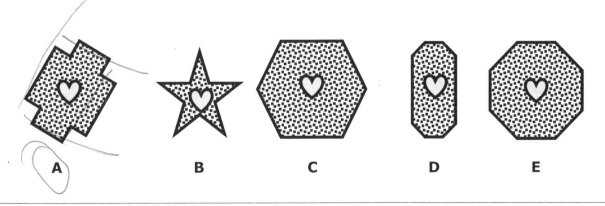

| A | B | C | D | E |

9.

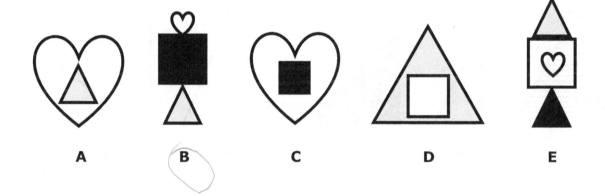

| A | B | C | D | E |

10.

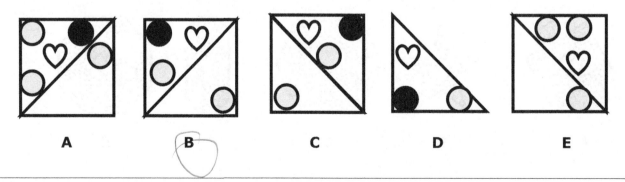

| A | B | C | D | E |

11.

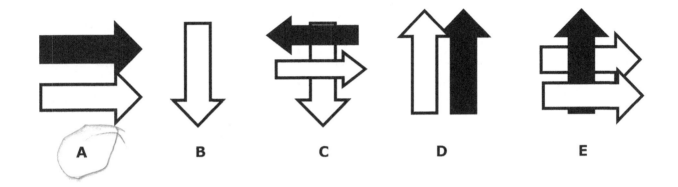

A   B   C   D   E

12.

   B   C   D   

A   B   C   D   E

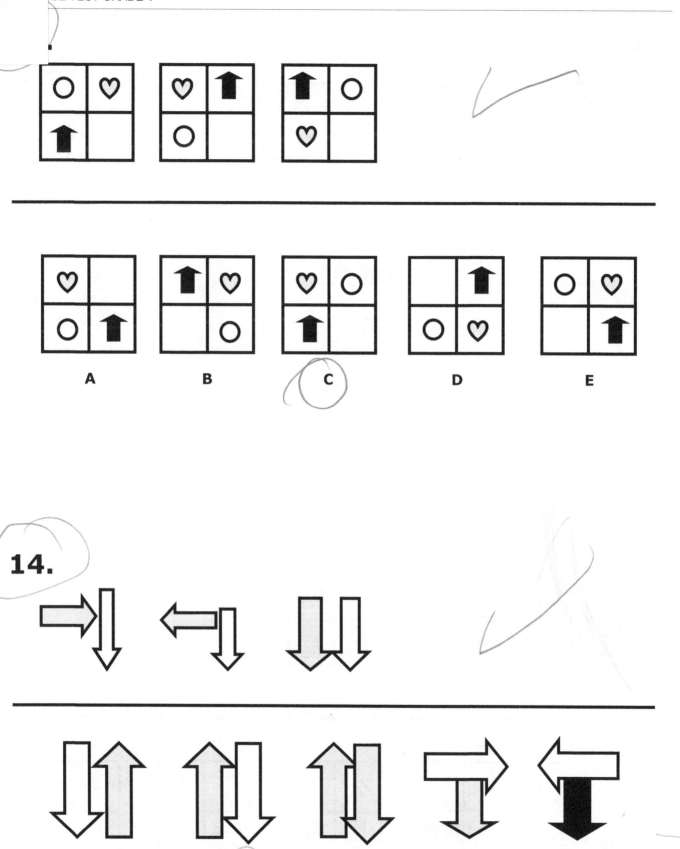

14.

15.

A   B   C   D   E

16.

A   B   C   D   E

17.

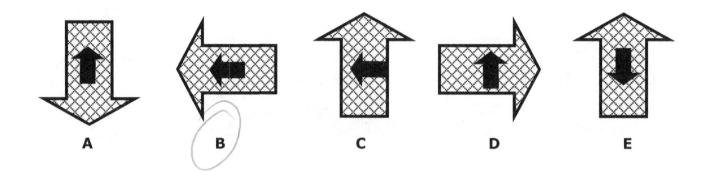

| A | B | C | D | E |

18.

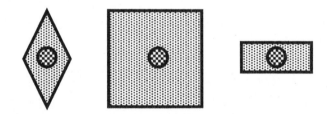

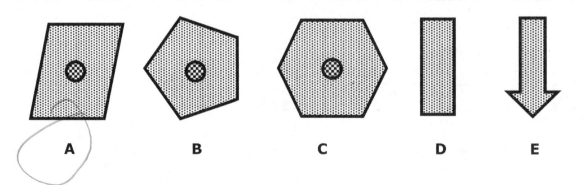

| A | B | C | D | E |

19.

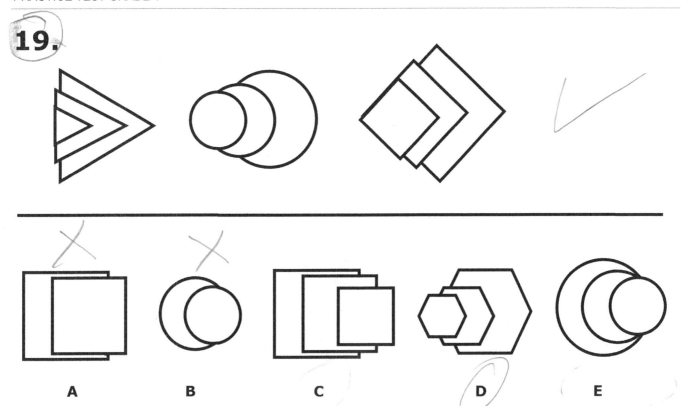

A   B   C   D   E

20.

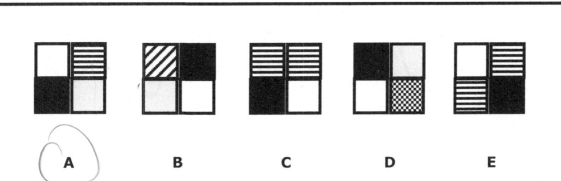

A   B   C   D   E

21.

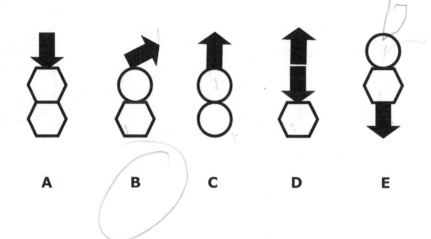

| A | B | C | D | E |

22.

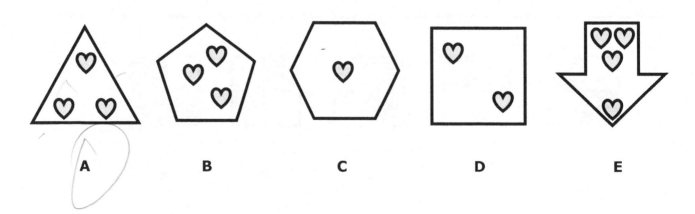

| A | B | C | D | E |

Paper Folding

Students need to determine the appearance of a perforated and folded sheet of paper, once opened.

Example

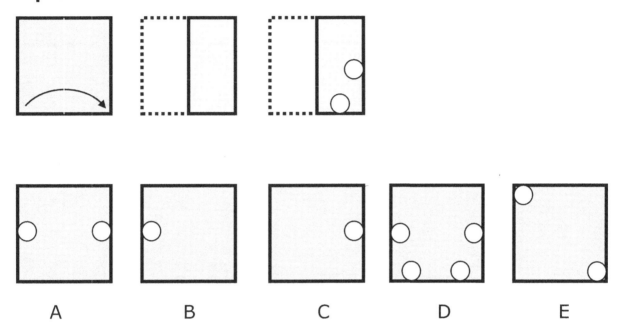

The figures at the top represent a square piece of paper being folded, and the last of these figures has two holes on it.

One of the lower five figures shows where the perforations will be when the paper is fully unfolded. You have to understand which of these images is the right one.

First, the paper was folded horizontally, from left to right.

Then, two holes were punched out. Therefore, when the paper is unfolded the holes will mirror on the left and right side of the sheet. The right answer is "D".

Tips for Paper Folding

The best way to get ready for these challenging questions is to practice. The patterns that show up on the test can confuse students, so the demonstration of folding and unfolding real paper can be very helpful.

1.

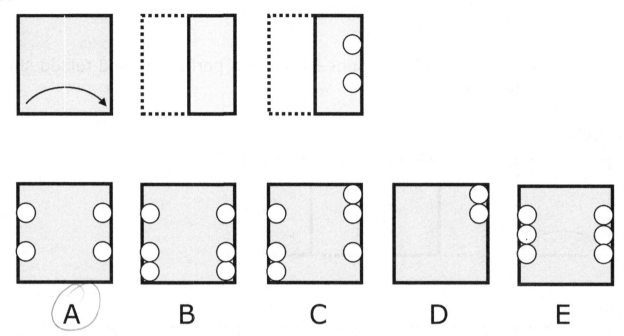

2.

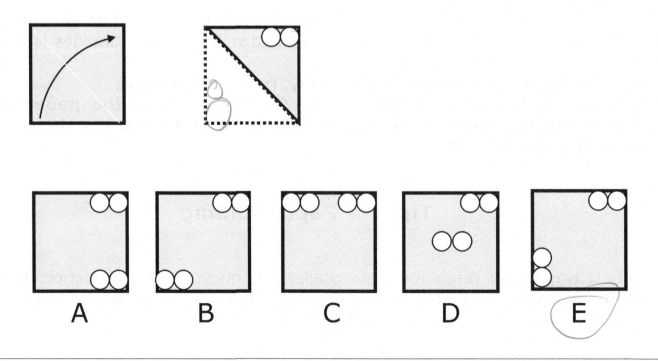

3.

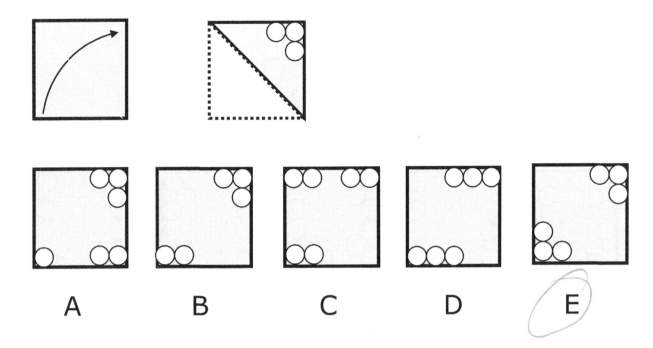

A   B   C   D   E

4.

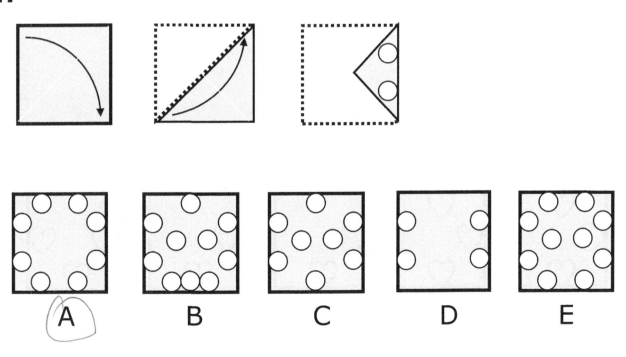

A   B   C   D   E

5.

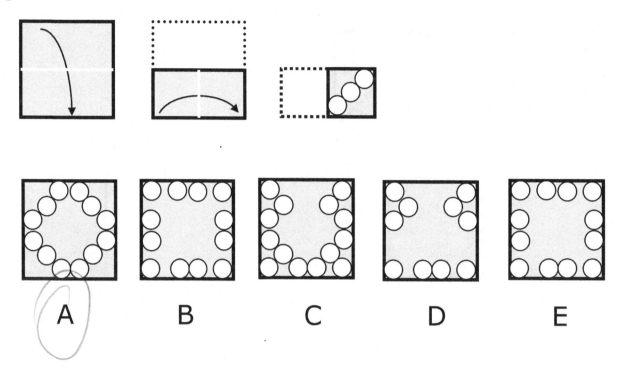

6.

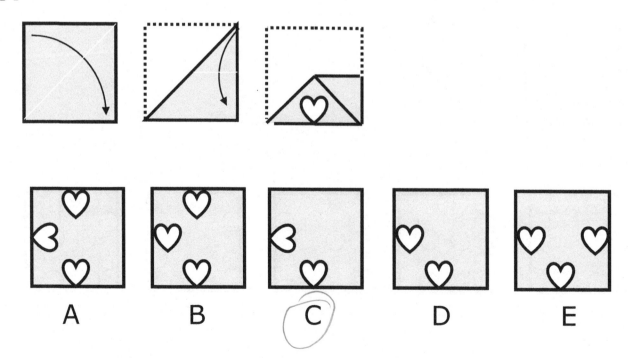

7.

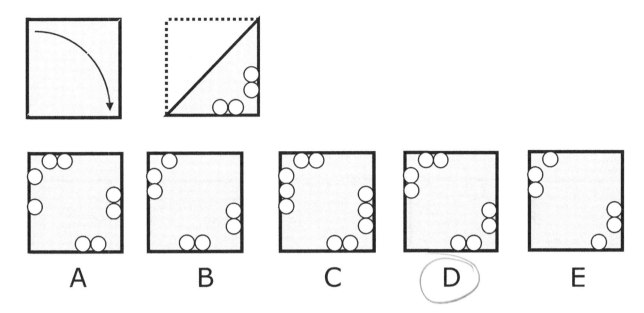

8.

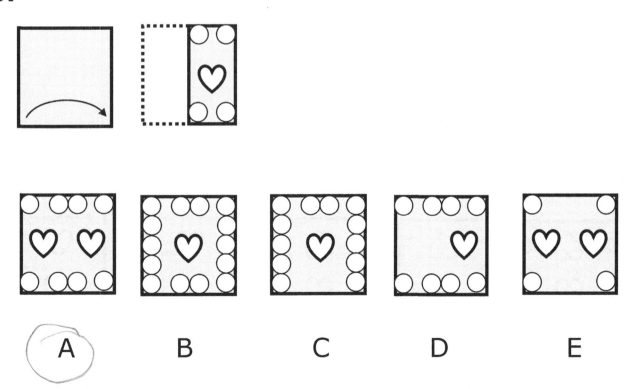

9.

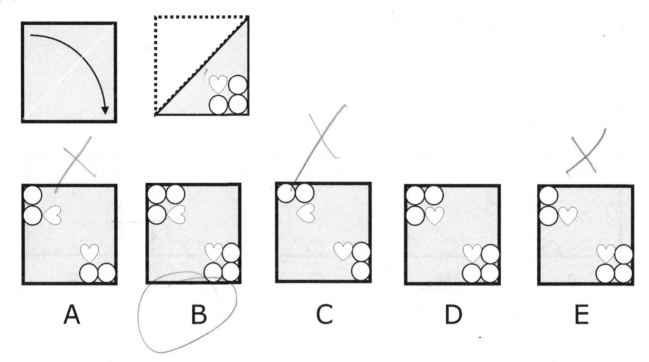

10.

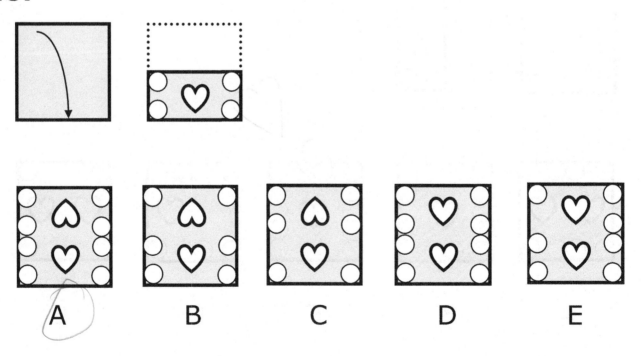

11.

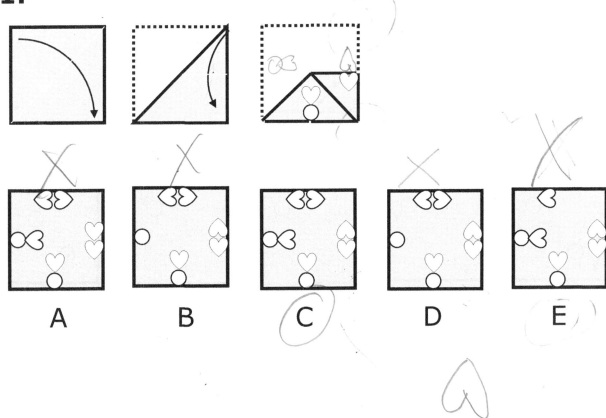

A   B   C   D   E

12.

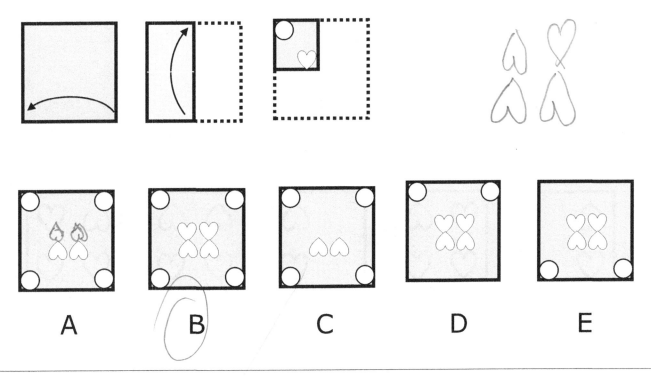

A   B   C   D   E

13.

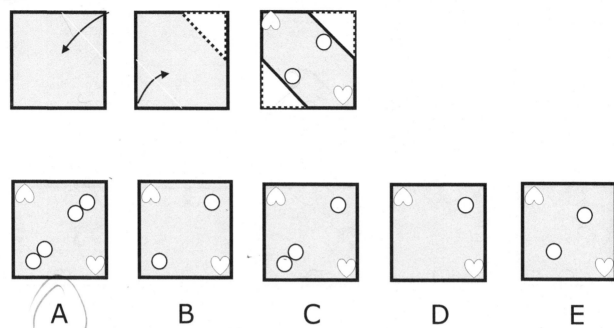

14.

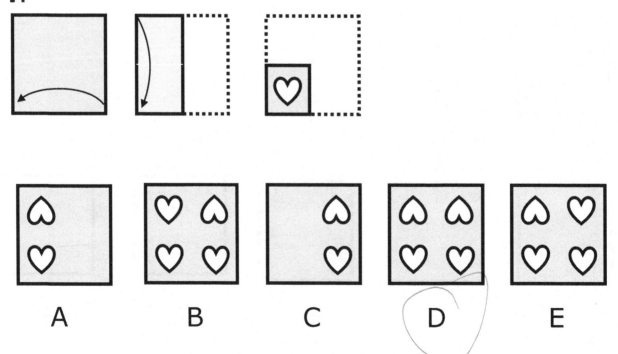

15.

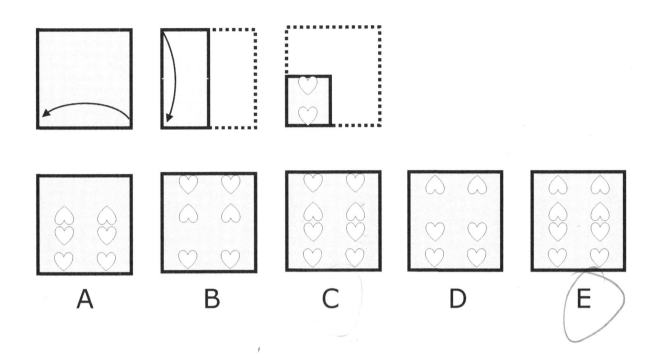

16.

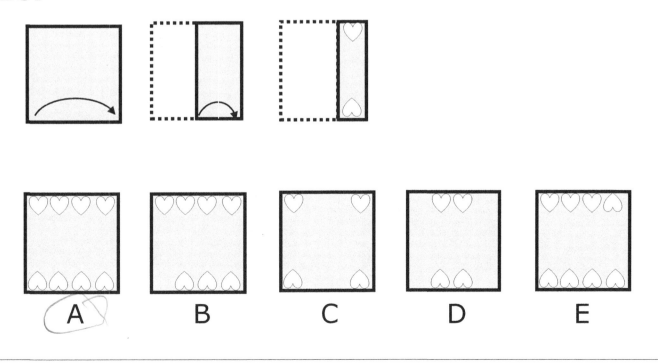

QUANTITATIVE BATTERY GRADE 4

This section introduces abstract reasoning and problem-solving skills to learners and is one of the most challenging sections in the test.

Number Puzzle

Students are required to solve basic mathematical equations. An equation says that two things are equal. It will have an equals sign "=" like this:

$$8 + 1 = 12 - 3$$

The equation says that what is on the left (4 + 2) is equal to what is on the right (10 − 4).

Example 1

$$? - 10 = 3$$

A 11   B 13   C 2   D 5   E 6

- The right side of the equal sign is 3. Which answer should be given in place of the question mark, so that the left side of the equal is also 3?

13 - 10 = 3; 3=3

The right answer is "B".

Example 2

$$? + \blacklozenge = 12$$

$$\blacklozenge = 7$$

A 2   **B** 14   **C** 5   **D** 9   **E** 7

? + 7= 12; 5+7=12; 12=12; the right answer is "C".

Tips for Number Puzzle

- Deeply understand the meaning of "equal", as the purpose is to provide the missing information that will make the two parts of the equation the same.
- Train yourself to solve simple basic equations.
- Practice with numbers and problem solving.

1.

$$? - 4 = 15$$

A 19   **B** 12   **C** 1   **D** 17   **E** 18

2.

$$? + \blacklozenge = 19$$

$$\blacklozenge = 9$$

A 11   **B** 12   **C** 10   **D** 18   **E** 14

3.

$$? + 14 = \blacklozenge$$

$$\blacklozenge = 26$$

A 1   **B** 12   **C** 0   **D** 20   **E** 11

4.

$$? \times 2 = \blacklozenge + 6$$

$$\blacklozenge = 14$$

A 11   **B** 9   **C** 10   **D** 1   **E** 16

5.

$$? - 3 = \blacklozenge + 1$$

$$\blacklozenge = 99$$

A 20   **B** 1   **C** 3   **D** 12   **E** 103

6.

$$9 + 5 = 24 - ?$$

A 20   **B** 10   **C** 11   **D** 6   **E** 4

7.

$$20 = 50 - 11 - ?$$

A 19   **B** 20   **C** 21   **D** 18   **E** 10

8.

$$12 = 48 - 40 + ?$$

A 11   **B** 5   **C** 7   **D** 6   **E** 4

9. $$51 = 1 + 20 + ?$$

A 31   **B** 35   **C** 28   **D** 30   **E** 12

10.

$$70 - 20 = 80 - ?$$

A 25   **B** 28   **C** 31   **D** 30   **E** 18

11.

$$10 + 20 = 41 - ?$$

A 11   **B** 16   **C** 20   **D** 14   **E** 8

12.

$$80 - 10 = 100 - ?$$

A 19   **B** 30   **C** 20   **D** 32   **E** 14

13.

$$? = \blacklozenge + 12$$

$$\blacklozenge = 40$$

A 53   **B** 60   **C** 68   **D** 55   **E** 52

14.

$$? = \blacklozenge \times 3$$

$$\blacklozenge = 9$$

A 30   **B** 10   **C** 27   **D** 25   **E** 31

15.

$$? \ = \ \blacklozenge \ X \ 2$$

$$\blacklozenge \ = \ 8$$

A 18   **B** 16   **C** 19   **D** 20   **E** 14

16.

$$? \ = \ \blacklozenge \ + \ 7$$

$$8 \ = \ \blacklozenge \ - \ \bullet$$

$$\bullet \ = \ 2$$

A 14   **B** 18   **C** 17   **D** 20   **E** 10

Number Analogies

In this session, you will see two pairs of numbers and then a number without its pair. The first two pairs of numbers are correlated in some way. Try to find out the correlation between the numbers within each of the pairs. Choose an answer that gives you the third pair of numbers, related to each other in the same way.

Example

[8 → 4]   [6 → 3]   [20 → ?]

A 2   **B** 19   **C** 10   **D** 7   **E** 6

- In the first two sets, you have 8 and 4; 6 and 3. Both numbers (8 and 6), are divided by 2 (8:2=4; 6:2=3).
- Apply the same rule to the number 20.

20 : 2 = 10. The right answer is "C".

Tips for Number Analogies

- Step 1: acquire all the information from the two given pairs (relationships, sums, subtractions, etc.).
- Step 2: apply the same rules, relations, formulas that you correctly identified in step 1.
- Step 3: double-check that the rule has been properly applied.

1.

[5 → 9]   [6 → 10]   [15 → ?]

A 18   **B** 19   **C** 15   **D** 12   **E** 14

2.

[4 → 8]   [3 → 6]   [14 → ?]

A 28   **B** 10   **C** 18   **D** 29   **E** 30

3.

[11 → 7]   [8 → 4]   [90 → ?]

A 89   **B** 86   **C** 80   **D** 5   **E** 91

4.

[24 → 8]   [9 → 3]   [36 → ?]

A 13   **B** 16   **C** 16   **D** 12   **E** 21

5.

[2 → 2]   [10 → 18]   [20 → ?]

A 25   **B** 12   **C** 36   **D** 35   **E** 38

6.

[2 → 22]   [4 → 44]   [3 → ?]

A 33   **B** 35   **C** 30   **D** 21   **E** 41

7.

[4 → 16]   [1 → 4]   [5 → ?]

A 12   **B** 17   **C** 20   **D** 19   **E** 25

8.

[45 → 35]   [28 → 18]   [10 → ?]

A 10   **B** 2   **C** 5   **D** 0   **E** 1

9.

[18 → 3]   [36 → 6]   [6 → ?]

A 1   **B** 12   **C** 3   **D** 14   **E** 24

10.

[12 → 21]   [31 → 40]   [10 → ?]

A 18   **B** 10   **C** 14   **D** 16   **E** 19

11.

[20 → 4]   [35 → 7]   [10 → ?]

A 1   **B** 3   **C** 2   **D** 5   **E** 9

12.

[8 → 40]   [11 → 55]   [9 → ?]

A 45   **B** 46   **C** 35   **D** 40   **E** 28

13.

[77 → 11]   [42 → 6]   [14 → ?]

A 3   **B** 5   **C** 7   **D** 2   **E** 12

14.

[18 → 6]   [30 → 18]   [13 → ?]

A 2   **B** 4   **C** 1   **D** 10   **E** 9

15.

[19 → 13]   [20 → 14]   [45 → ?]

A 28   **B** 39   **C** 33   **D** 29   **E** 34

16.

[12 → 144]   [2 → 24]   [3 → ?]

A 10   **B** 12   **C** 35   **D** 36   **E** 37

17.

[39 ➝ 13]   [9 ➝ 3]   [81 ➝ ?]

 A 27   **B** 19   **C** 30   **D** 13   **E** 24

18.   ×3 ×4
        +2 −3   ×4
                                     −3
[5 ➝ 17]   [4 ➝ 13]   [9 ➝ ?]

A 39   **B** 33   **C** 36   **D** 21   **E** 18

Number Series

Students are provided with a sequence of numbers that follow a pattern. They are required to identify which number should come next in the sequence.

Example 1

2   4   6   8   ?

A 10   **B** 12   **C** 11   **D** 6   **E** 8

- It's easy to realize that each number in the sequence increases by 2. 2+2=4; 4+2=6; 6+2=8; etc.
- Apply the same rule to the number 8.

8 + 2 = 10. The right answer is "A".

Example 2

2   4   3   5   4   ?

A 5   **B** 1   **C** 11   **D** 10   **E** 6

- The sequence follows the rule: +2, -1, +2, -1, +2, etc. 2+2=4; 4-1=3; 3+2=5; 5-1=4; etc.
- Apply the same rule to the number 4.

4 + 2 = 6 The right answer is "E".

Tips for Number Series

- To correctly answer these questions, the student will need to be able to identify the patterns in a sequence of numbers and provide the missing item. Therefore, it is important to practice, working with sequences of numbers.

1.

    5   **7**   **9**   **11**   **?**

A 13   **B** 11   **C** 10   **D** 9   **E** 15

2.

    20   **18**   **16**   **14**   **12**   **?**

A 11   **B** 12   **C** 10   **D** 18   **E** 1

3.

-2 +1 -2 +1 -2

    4   **2**   **3**   **1**   **2**   **?**

A 1   **B** 10   **C** 3   **D** 5   **E** 0

4.

+5 -2 +5 -2 +5 -2 +5

    10   **15**   **13**   **18**   **16**   **21**   **19**   **?**

A 30   **B** 24   **C** 22   **D** 11   **E** 18

5.

+1   +2   +3

10   11   13   16   ?

A 29   **B** 12   **C** 25   **D** 22   **E** 20

6.

−1 +10 −1 +10 −1 +10

1   0   10   9   19   18   ?

A 29   **B** 31   **C** 28   **D** 29   **E** 30

7.

5   0   5   0   5   ?

A 1   **B** 15   **C** 3   **D** 5   **E** 0

8.

−3 +1 −3 +1 −3 +1

12   9   10   7   8   5   ?

A 7   **B** 9   **C** 6   **D** 8   **E** 10

9.

66   60   54   48   42   ?

(handwritten: −6 −6 −6 −6 −6)

A 36   **B** 33   **C** 42   **D** 45   **E** 30

10.

2   3   8   9   14   15   ?

(handwritten: +1 +5 +1 +5 +1 +5)

A 18   **B** 22   **C** 24   **D** 19   **E** 20

11.

7   10   9   12   11   14   ?

(handwritten: +3 −1 +3 −1 +3 −1)

A 12   **B** 13   **C** 11   **D** 18   **E** 19

12.

3   13   23   33   43   53   ?

A 70   **B** 63   **C** 53   **D** 33   **E** 38

13.

| 4 | 7 | 3 | 6 | 2 | 5 | ? |

A 9   **B** 10   **C** 2   **D** 3   **E** 1

14.

0.1   1.1   2.1   3.1   4.1   5.1   ?

A 6.2   **B** 6.1   **C** 6   **D** 4.3   **E** 7.3

15.

0.05   0.08   0.11   0.14   0.17   ?

A 0.09   **B** 0.1   **C** 0.35   **D** 0.20   **E** 0.3

16.

50   47   44   41   38   35   ?

A 32   **B** 28   **C** 36   **D** 30   **E** 31

17.

2.5 +4 2.9 +4 3.3 +4 3.7 +4 4.1 +4 4.5 +4 **?**

A 4.5   **B** 5,5   **C** 6   **D** 4.9   **E** 5

18.

−5 4   3.95   3.9   3.85   3.8   3.75   **?**

A 3.7   **B** 3   **C** 4   **D** 3.2   **E** 3.1

ANSWER KEY FOR PRACTICE TEST GRADE 4

Verbal Analogies Practice Test Grade 4
p.209

1.
Answer: option E
Explanation: a blind person cannot see the light; a dumb person cannot speak.

2.
Answer: option C
Explanation: meter is a measure of a distance; liter is a measure of a liquid.

3.
Answer: option A
Explanation: stomachache is a stomach disorder; conjunctivitis is an eye disorder.

4.
Answer: option B
Explanation: iron is a metal; quartz is a mineral.

5.
Answer: option D
Explanation: a fork is used to eat; a car is used to travel.

6.
Answer: option D
Explanation: finger is a part of hand; pupil is a part of eye.

7.
Answer: option B
Explanation: a rose is a type of flower; a pine is a type of tree.

8.

Answer: option E

Explanation: a wheel is a part of a car; a hand is a part of a body.

9.

Answer: option B

Explanation: gasoline is a fuel; helium is a gas.

10.

Answer: option C

Explanation: something that is powerless lacks efficacy; something that is explicit lacks ambiguity.

11.

Answer: option A

Explanation: the opposite of wretched is cheerful; the opposite of innocuous is dangerous.

12.

Answer: option B

Explanation: a characteristic of a labyrinth is to be complicated; a characteristic of an enigma is to be mysterious.

13.

Answer: option B

Explanation: neutral is synonymous with indifferent; lazy is synonymous with indolent.

14.

Answer: option D

Explanation: avarice is the opposite of generosity; jeopardy is the opposite of security.

15.

Answer: option B

Explanation: a fin is part of a fish; a wing is a part of a hen.

16.

Answer: option B

Explanation: a characteristic of a lion is strength; a characteristic of a cat is agility.

17.

Answer: option E

Explanation: a brush is used to paint; a straw is used to drink.

18.

Answer: option A

Explanation: hockey is a sport; chemistry is a science.

19.

Answer: option B

Explanation: teeth are used to chew; legs are used to walk.

20.

Answer: option D

Explanation: someone who is selfish lacks compassion; someone who is childish lacks maturity.

21.

Answer: option C

Explanation: a "doctor" works inside a "hospital," similar to how a "cashier" works inside a "supermarket."

22.

Answer: option E

Explanation: "slept" is the past tense expression of the verb "sleep"; "bought" is the past tense expression of "buy.

23.

Answer: option B

Explanation: lenient is the opposite of strict; punctual is the opposite of laggard.

24.

Answer: option B

Explanation: an ingredient is part of a recipe; a roof is part of a house.

Verbal Classification Practice Test Grade 4
p.216

1.
Answer: option E
Explanation: date, day, month, year are parts of a calendar.

2.
Answer: option C
Explanation: carrot, ginger, lettuce, and celery are vegetables.

3.
Answer: option A
Explanation: Mercury, Venus, Earth and Mars are planets.

4.
Answer: option B
Explanation: chair, sofa, table, and wardrobe are types of furnitures.

5.
Answer: option D
Explanation: sister, brother, father, and mother have blood relations.

6.
Answer: option D
Explanation: lion, cheetah, tiger, and leopard belong to the cat family.

7.
Answer: option B
Explanation: speedboat, sailboat, kayak, and yacht are means of transport by water.

8.
Answer: option E
Explanation: dragonfly, butterfly, ant, and ladybug are insects.

9.
Answer: option B
Explanation: wheat, maize, rye and quinoa are types of cereals.

10.
Answer: option C
Explanation: Nigeria, Egypt, Ethiopia, and Tanzania are states in Africa.

11.
Answer: option A
Explanation: coke, milk, tea and juice are liquids.

12.
Answer: option B
Explanation: frog, toad, salamander, and newt are amphibians.

13.
Answer: option C
Explanation: sea lion, dolphin, whale and porpoise are acquatic marine mammals.

14.
Answer: option A
Explanation: crocodile, iguana, gecko and anaconda are reptiles.

15.

Answer: option C

Explanation: akita, beagle, boxer, and bulldog are dog breeds.

16.

Answer: option A

Explanation: buy, sell, eat and create are verbs.

17.

Answer: option E

Explanation: Hindi, Japanese, Portuguese are languages; Russian is also a language.

18.

Answer: option B

Explanation: hexagon, rhombus, octagon are plane figures; square is also a plan figure.

19.

Answer: option C

Explanation: big, colossal, fat and immense are adjectives related to size.

20.

Answer: option A

Explanation: bedroom, laundry, living room and kitchen are rooms of the house.

Sentence Completion Practice Test Grade 4
p.222

1.
Answer: option C
Explanation: safe=protected from or not exposed to danger or risk.

2.
Answer: option A
Explanation: cage= a structure of bars or wires in which some animals are confined.

3.
Answer: option D
Explanation: joy=a feeling of great pleasure and happiness.

4.
Answer: option C
Explanation: euphoria = a state of intense happiness and self-confidence.

5.
Answer: option B
Explanation: see= perceive with the eyes; discern visually.

6.
Answer: option C
Explanation: tragic= causing or characterized by extreme distress or sorrow.

7.
Answer: option D
Explanation: learn= gain or acquire knowledge of or skill in (something) by study, experience, or being taught.

8.

Answer: option C

Explanation: damage = a bad effect on something.

9.

Answer: option B

Explanation: receive = to be given something.

10.

Answer: option E

Explanation: already= used to say that something has been done before and does not need doing again.

11.

Answer: option C

Explanation: build =to construct something.

12.

Answer: option A

Explanation: impressive=something that is impressive makes you admire it because it is very good, large, important etc.

13.

Answer: option D

Explanation: good = of a high standard or quality.

14.

Answer: option D

Explanation: fade=to gradually disappear.

15.

Answer: option E

Explanation: create=to make something exist that did not exist before.

16.

Answer: option C

Explanation: read music = to look at written notes and understand what they mean.

17.

Answer: option D

Explanation: children may improperly use medicines.

18.

Answer: option E

Explanation: key (adjective) = very important or necessary.

19.

Answer: option C

Explanation: disease = an illness which affects a person.

20.

Answer: option E

Explanation: bad = unpleasant or likely to cause problems.

Figure Matrices Practice Test Grade 4
p.231

1.
Answer: option A
Explanation: the right shapes of each box change position. In the upper right box, the grey square goes down; the white heart goes up. In the lower right box, the heart goes down and the circle goes up. Left shapes in each box don't change position.

2.
Answer: option C
Explanation: smaller shapes become grey; larger shapes become white.

3.
Answer: option D
Explanation: the figure in the middle is removed.

4.
Answer: option D
Explanation: the upper shape goes inside the lower shape.

5.
Answer: option B
Explanation: (four pointed star: five pointed star) = (six pointed star: seven pointed star).

6.
Answer: option B
Explanation: the right shape has one more side than the one on the left.

7.
Answer: option E
Explanation: the left figure rotates by 180 degrees and changes color.

8.
Answer: option D
Explanation: the figure in the middle is removed.

9.
Answer: option B
Explanation: the larger shape becomes black; the smaller shape becomes white.

10.
Answer: option D
Explanation: the lower shape is eliminated.

11.
Answer: option C
Explanation: the shapes on the left change size; the top figures goes inside the lower ones.

12.
Answer: option C
Explanation: half width, same color.

13.
Answer: option A
Explanation: the larger shape is eliminated and the inside shape becomes black.

14.
Answer: option E
Explanation: the circles are removed; the larger shapes become black.

15.

Answer: option B

Explanation: the figures on the left are placed in a circle.

16.

Answer: option E

Explanation: 180-degree rotation and the color becomes grey.

17.

Answer: option C

Explanation: addition of a white arrow over the figures on the left.

18.

Answer: option E

Explanation: the left triangle is removed.

19.

Answer: option A

Explanation: combos of same shapes, one on top of the other (to the left), one inside the other (to the right).

20.

Answer: option C

Explanation: the shape within moves up.

21.

Answer: option B

Explanation: the right and left figures have the same number of sides.

22.

Answer: option B

Explanation: the white arrow is removed. The black arrow rotates by 90 degrees clockwise.

Figure Classification Practice Test Grade 4
p.240

1.
Answer: option A
Explanation: white four-sided shapes.

2.
Answer: option E
Explanation: larger shapes and smaller inside figures have the same number of sides.

3.
Answer: option E
Explanation: the figures on the top have one more side than the larger figures.

4.
Answer: option D
Explanation: one vertical line and one horizontal line inside each shape; one octagon and one heart next to each other.

5.
Answer: option A
Explanation: four-sided shapes, same color.

6.
Answer: option D
Explanation: four-sided grey shapes divided into two parts.

7.

Answer: option E

Explanation: triangles of the same size and color.

8.

Answer: option A

Explanation: twelve-sided shapes; same color, 1 heart inside each shape.

9.

Answer: option B

Explanation: combos of grey triangle, black square and white heart.

10.

Answer: option B

Explanation: a black circle, a grey circle and a white heart lie on the left side of a diagonal; a grey circle lies on the right side of a diagonal.

11.

Answer: option A

Explanation: a black arrow and a white arrow; the black arrow is above the white arrow.

12.

Answer: option A

Explanation: in the matching sub squares, the arrows have the same color.

13.

Answer: option C

Explanation: the heart, circle, and arrow change position, but the lower right square stays empty.

14.

Answer: option B

Explanation: a grey arrow and a white arrow; the white arrow is to the right side of the gray one.

15.
Answer: option B
Explanation: rounded shapes with a white heart inside.

16.
Answer: option A
Explanation: same rotated figures, same sizes, same colors.

17.
Answer: option B
Explanation: two arrows, one inside the other, pointing in the same direction.

18.
Answer: option A
Explanation: four-sided shapes in the same color with one circle inside.

19.
Answer: option D
Explanation: three figures; the size of designs is increasing gradually from the left to right.

20.
Answer: option A
Explanation: four squares in every box, each having a specific color, but in different positions.

21.
Answer: option B
Explanation: combos of circle, hexagon, and arrow; the arrow must be on the top.

22.
Answer: option A
Explanation: in each shape, there are as many grey hearts as there are sides in the figure.

Paper Folding Practice Test Grade 4
p.252

1.
Answer: option A

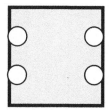

2.
Answer: option E

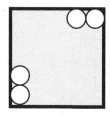

3.
Answer: option E

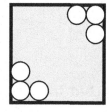

4.
Answer: option A

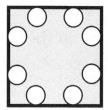

5.
Answer: option A

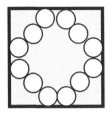

6.
Answer: option C

7
Answer: option D

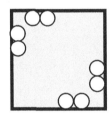

8.
Answer: option A

9.
Answer: option B

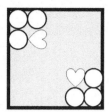

10.
Answer: option A

11.
Answer: option C

12.
Answer: option B

13.
Answer: option A

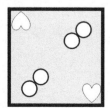

14.
Answer: option D

15.
Answer: option E

16.
Answer: option A

Number Puzzle Practice Test Grade 4
p.263

1.
Answer: option A
Explanation: 19-4=15; 15=15

2.
Answer: option C
Explanation: 10+9=19; 19=19

3.
Answer: option B
Explanation: 12+14=26; 26=26

4.
Answer: option C
Explanation: 10X2=14+6; 20=20

5.
Answer: option E
Explanation: 103-3=99+1; 100=100

6.
Answer: option B
Explanation: 9+5=24-10; 14=14

7.
Answer: option A
Explanation: 20=50-11-19; 20=50-30; 20=20

8.
Answer: option E
Explanation: 12=48-40+4; 12=8+4; 12=12

9.
Answer: option D
Explanation: 51=1+20+30; 51=21+30; 51=51

10.
Answer: option D
Explanation: 70-20=80-30; 50=50

11.
Answer: option A
Explanation: 10+20=41-11; 30=30

12.
Answer: option B
Explanation: 80-10 =100-30; 70=70

13.
Answer: option E
Explanation: 52=40+12; 52=52

14.
Answer: option C
Explanation: 27=9X3; 27=27

15.
Answer: option B
Explanation: 16=8X2; 16=16

16.
Answer: option C
Explanation: $\blacklozenge$ = 8+2; $\blacklozenge$=10; 17=10+7; 17=17

Number Analogies Practice Test Grade 4
p.269

1.
Answer: option B
Explanation: 5+4=9   6+4=10   15+4=19

2.
Answer: option A
Explanation: 4X2=8   3X2=6   14X2=28

3.
Answer: option B
Explanation: 11-4=7   8-4=4   90-4=86

4.
Answer: option D
Explanation: 24:3=8   9:3=3   36:3=12

5.
Answer: option E
Explanation: 2X2=4; 4-2=2   10X2=20; 20-2=18   20X2=40; 40-2=38

6.
Answer: option A
Explanation: 2X11=22   4X11=44   3X11=33

7.
Answer: option C
Explanation: 4X4=16; 1X4=4; 5X4=20;

8.
Answer: option D
Explanation: 45-10=35   28-10=18   10-10=0

9.
Answer: option A
Explanation: 18:6=3   36:6=6   6:6=1

10.
Answer: option E
Explanation: 12+9=21   31+9=40   10+9=19

11.
Answer: option C
Explanation: 20:5=4   35:5=7   10:5=2

12.
Answer: option A
Explanation: 8X5=40   11X5=55   9X5=45

13.
Answer: option D
Explanation: 77:7=11   42:7=6   14:7=2

14.
Answer: option C
Explanation: 18-12=6   30-12=18   13-12=1

15.
Answer: option B
Explanation: 19-6=13   20-6=14   45-6=39

16.
Answer: option D
Explanation: 12X12=144   2X12=24   3X12=36

17.
Answer: option A
Explanation: 39:3=13   9:3=3   81:3=27

18.
Answer: option B
Explanation: 5X4=20; 20-3=17   4X4=16; 16-3=13
                9X4=36; 36-3=33

Number Series Practice Test Grade 4
p.275

1.
Answer: option A
Explanation: +2, +2, +2, +2, etc. 5+2=7; 7+2=9; 9+2=11; 11+2=13

2.
Answer: option C
Explanation: -2, -2, -2, -2, -2, etc.

3.
Answer: option E
Explanation: -2, +1, -2, +1, -2

4.
Answer: option B
Explanation: +5, -2, +5, -2, +5, -2, +5, etc.

5.
Answer: option E
Explanation: +1, +2, +3, +4, etc.

6.
Answer: option C
Explanation: -1, +10, -1, +10, -1, +10, etc.

7.
Answer: option E
Explanation: -5, +5, -5, +5, -5, etc.

8.
Answer: option C
Explanation: -3, +1, -3, +1, -3, +1, etc.

9.
Answer: option A
Explanation: -6, -6, -6, -6, -6, etc.

10.
Answer: option E
Explanation: +1, +5, +1, +5, +1, +5, etc.

11.
Answer: option B
Explanation: +3, -1, +3, -1, +3, -1, etc.

12.
Answer: option B
Explanation: +10, +10, +10, +10, +10, +10, etc.

13.
Answer: option E
Explanation: +3, -4, +3, -4, +3, -4, etc.

14.
Answer: option B
Explanation: +1, +1, +1, +1, +1, +1, etc.

15.
Answer: option D
Explanation: +0.03, +0.03, +0.03, +0.03, +0.03, +0.03, etc.

16.
Answer: option A
Explanation: -3, -3, -3, -3, -3, -3, etc.

17.
Answer: option D
Explanation: +0.4, +0.4, +0.4, +0.4, +0.4, +0.4, etc.

18.
Answer: option A
Explanation: -0.05, -0.05, -0.05, -0.05, -0.05, -0.05, etc.

HOW TO DOWNLOAD 54 BONUS QUESTIONS

(FOR GRADE 3 GO TO PAGE 203)

Thank you for reading this book, we hope you really enjoyed it and found it very helpful.

PLEASE LEAVE US A REVIEW ON THE WEBSITE WHERE YOU PURCHASED THIS BOOK!

By leaving a review, you give us the opportunity to improve our work.

A GIFT FOR YOU!
FREE ONLINE ACCESS TO 54 BONUS PRACTICE QUESTIONS.

Follow this link:

https://www.skilledchildren.com/cogat-test-prep-grade-4.php
You will find a PDF to download: please insert this PASSWORD: 220867

Nicole Howard and the SkilledChildren.com Team

www.skilledchildren.com

Made in the USA
Monee, IL
05 January 2023